The Colours of South Yorkshire

Bob Telfer – Richard Simons

Image work by Michael Eyre

Capital Transport

Acknowledgements

The images presented here span a period of just over two decades from the 1950s, when technological advancements led to colour photography becoming more affordable, through to 1974 when so much in the local transport scene was lost. We are immensely grateful to the photographers who had the foresight to record what they saw and have now made the results available for inclusion here; this is really their book. Sadly several are no longer with us, and we must thank their representatives who have given us access to their work. We believe the photographs have been correctly credited to the photographer or copyright holder – our apologies to anyone whose work has been wrongly attributed.

We should also thank those who kindly provided assistance in various ways, including Don Akrigg, Chris Aston, Roger Davies, Mike Fenton, Peter Greaves, Mike Greenwood, John Kaye, Iain MacGregor, Eric Moy, Paul Fox and members of the Sheffield Transport Study Group, especially Tom Robinson and Graham Hague.

The high quality of the reproduction of the images in the book is entirely due to patient and painstaking work by Michael Eyre, whose ability to bring tired images back to life is astonishing. Also we must thank Jim Whiting and his team at Capital Transport for giving us the opportunity to put this book together.

The authors have drawn information from a multitude of sources – particularly useful have been various publications by the Omnibus Society and PSV Circle, and works by Alan Hilton and Charles Hall.

We took a decision not to duplicate any of the contents of *The Colours of West Yorkshire* and have kept to a minimum coverage of operators illustrated in that volume. Thus there are no images of operators such as County Motors, United Services and Baddeley Brothers and only brief coverage of West Riding and South Yorkshire Motors.

We have tried to offer as varied a selection of views as possible but please remember that half a century or more ago many of the photographers would not have had their own transport – so it is no surprise that they favoured the more accessible locations, where there was invariably so much variety on offer.

Front cover: Sheffield invested heavily in new buses throughout the 1950s, replacing earlier buses as well as almost the whole of the tram system, which had been largely intact at the start of the decade and finally closed in 1960. AECs and Leylands were chosen throughout, and for the 1954 phase of the tram-replacement programme 56 Weymann-bodied Leyland PD2s were bought. 704 was one of them. It is pictured in Sheaf Street operating as a duplicate to the Castleton service as far as Fox House, a gateway to the Peak District and a very popular weekend destination. An A fleet bus on a short working of a Category B service operated jointly with North Western highlights the complexity of the Sheffield operation. *Geoffrey Morant*

Back cover: It is perhaps surprising that few of London Transport's surplus RTs found their way into South Yorkshire fleets. One that did was HLX 142, formerly RT155, an early example that had entered service in the capital in 1947. By the time it passed to Leon in 1958, it had gained the Weymann body originally fitted to RT416. It is pulling out of Glasgow Paddocks Bus Station in September 1964 on its regular service to Finningley. The between-decks advertisement for Leon's coaching activities includes a reasonable representation of the company's Burlingham Seagull bodied Daimler Freeline, pride of the fleet. Two of the Corporation's Leyland PD3s are visible in the background. *Ken Jubb*

Frontispiece: Doncaster was remarkable for its independents. The variety of liveries and the individual purchasing policy of the various operators was fascinating. This view from August 1960 illustrates the variety to be seen on just one service – that to Rossington. Buses from the three independents that shared the service with the Corporation are standing just inside the entrance to Glasgow Paddocks Bus Station, each waiting to duplicate the service departure at its allocated departure time. In the foreground, in Rossie Motors' livery of light and dark green and cream, is Daimler CVD6 HWX 753 with bodyw... Barnard of Norwich. Also in full view in the red and cream livery of Don Motors is EDT 680, a Leyl... with bodywork constructed by Samlesbury. Just visible behind the Daimler, in the blue and cream livery of Blue Ensign is KDT 393, an AEC Regent III that was new to the Corporation in 1951 but sold off after just four years. *Geoff Warnes*

Contents

The book covers the municipal, company and independent operators based in what became the Metropolitan County of South Yorkshire together with brief coverage of the one municipal operator and five major company operators that worked into it. In addition to their buses most of the operators had sizeable coach fleets; in this book the focus is on the buses.

First published 2017

ISBN 978-185414-412-6

Published by and copyright
Capital Transport Publishing Ltd

www.capitaltransport.com

Printed in the EU

Images copyright of the photographers or owning bodies named herein

Introduction

The Metropolitan County of South Yorkshire came into being in April 1974, a result of a far-reaching restructuring of local government that swept away the historic Ridings of Yorkshire as well as the complex pattern of county boroughs and urban and rural districts that had existed since the 19th century. An immediate effect was the disappearance of municipal public transport.

Until then the area that included Sheffield, Barnsley, Doncaster, Rotherham and several smaller towns had formed part of the West Riding. Its staple industries were coal mining and metal-working, in contrast to the area just to the north (the new West Yorkshire) where wool and textiles dominated. Sheffield was synonymous with steel and cutlery production, although today it may be better known for sporting events and snooker championships. The rest of South Yorkshire will be less well known to many and we hope that this book will reveal something of its varied character.

Topographically, South Yorkshire is full of contrasts. In the west the Pennine moors, situated partly within the Peak District National Park, rise above 1,700 feet, yet in the east the fen-like flatlands beyond Doncaster are almost at sea level. These very different yet equally remote landscapes, where the nearest road can be three miles away, are virtually unpopulated – something of an enigma in an area designated as metropolitan. Between these extremes the terrain is varied, heavily urbanised in parts and pleasantly rural in others. During the period covered here, before the elimination of mining and the scaling back of heavy industry, vast areas were blighted and blackened but, with the exception of Sheffield and Rotherham, the main towns were separated by countryside, as they still are today.

Before 1974, when the newly created South Yorkshire Passenger Transport Executive embarked on its task of integration and co-ordination, the bus scene was as varied as the geography. This book celebrates that increasingly forgotten era, when the county boroughs of Doncaster, Rotherham and Sheffield each had their own municipal transport departments, there were two locally based subsidiaries of the British Electric Traction group and – perhaps best of all – around twenty local independent bus operators. Longer services from neighbouring counties brought even more variety, with buses in the municipal colours of Chesterfield, Halifax, Huddersfield and even Bradford, and in the liveries of major company operators – East Midland, Lincolnshire, North Western, Trent, West Riding and Yorkshire Woollen District.

At their peak the three municipal fleets accounted for over 1,000 buses, but municipal transport had begun in the tramway era. Sheffield led the way in 1896 and its system became legendary, with stylish modern cars being placed in service as late as 1952, yet the end came quickly after that, with services ceasing in 1960. Doncaster and Rotherham had trams by 1903 but their systems were shorter-lived. In part this was down to their adoption of trolleybuses, which also lasted into the 1960s, but after 1965 only the buses remained. Sheffield's joint venture with the railways (the Joint Omnibus Committee) meant that the city's buses could be seen far and wide, in places as diverse as Lancashire, Leeds and Lincolnshire. Extensive joint municipal operation was found in many major conurbations, but in South Yorkshire the 18-mile Sheffield – Rotherham – Doncaster service, started in 1927, was the only instance of the three undertakings working together. In fact this was Doncaster's only shared municipal operation, and Rotherham and Sheffield (or rather the JOC) worked together on just a handful of services.

Given the almost total lack of traffic, it is hard to believe that Doncaster 99 is heading out of town along the Great North Road. The early post-war fleet was sourced from several chassis manufacturers and 99 was one of five Bristol K6As with Roe bodies.
Geoff Warnes

Sheffield 36 is climbing out of the Don valley on Stocksbridge local service 357 to the Garden Village. New in 1968 it is an AEC Swift with dual door Park Royal bodywork. The Stockbridge steelworks is visible in the valley.
Martin Llewellyn

Barnsley followed a different path and despite the town's socialist leanings its buses were for decades provided almost entirely by private enterprise. The town's short tramway was opened in 1902 by a subsidiary of the London-based BET which in the late 1920s evolved into Yorkshire Traction. Helped a little by the demise of the Dearne District Light Railway, an eccentric municipal folly, it became the second largest bus operator in South Yorkshire, remaining in the private sector until BET sold its bus operations to the state in 1968.

The other local BET Company was Mexborough & Swinton, which had also started with trams (not then BET-owned), switched to trolleybuses in the 1920s and ran them until 1961. Under the National Bus Company, it was absorbed into Yorkshire Traction in 1969.

What really set South Yorkshire apart was the survival of local independent operators, with more than a dozen lasting into the 1970s and many of them clearly doing very nicely. No comparable area in the UK could match this. Doncaster was a particular stronghold of the independents and the town's Christ Church terminus was one of the most colourful in the country (and much photographed as a result). Some ran just one service, others a small group of services, but their importance to the local communities was beyond question.

Whilst some disappeared earlier, several others succumbed to the South Yorkshire Passenger Transport Executive's financial inducements in the 1970s and 1980s and only Leon of Finningley lasted into the new millennium. Two of the independents included in this volume, Booth & Fisher and Leon, do so because boundary changes brought their bases, originally in Derbyshire and Nottinghamshire respectively, within the 1974 South Yorkshire boundary.

Bus manufacturing played little part in Yorkshire's industrial base and with no chassis or engine makers there were no local allegiances or political pressures to skew buying policies. Operators bought whatever suited them best, frequently heavy-duty AECs and Leylands, although several other manufacturers also had a following. It was not until the 1960s that any one model found its way into the fleets of the five largest operators, and that was the Daimler Fleetline. Notably, all the local operators – even Sheffield with its famously arduous operating territory – seemed generally content to buy the manufacturers' standard offerings and did not feel the need, unlike many operators elsewhere, to develop their own specifications.

It was little different with bodywork. Charles Roe of Leeds was Yorkshire's only major manufacturer of bus bodies and they won their fair share of custom alongside the other major bodybuilders. At various times the products of Sheffield-based Cravens and Neepsend and Horbury-based Roberts had some success with orders, while other Yorkshire builders supplying the local market, albeit in small numbers, included Allsop, Barnaby, Cawood, Plaxton and Wilks & Meade.

Every fleet and distinctive livery illustrated within these pages is now nothing but a memory; the BET and Tilling group companies disappeared into the National Bus Company in 1969 (some later re-emerging in the privatised groups that replaced it), the local municipals were swallowed up by the South Yorkshire PTE in 1974 and the independents have gone without trace. The decades since deregulation in 1986 may have been at least as colourful but have lacked the continuity, stability and much of the pride which were taken for granted until the 1970s. But that's another story ....

In the early 1960s, Barnsley still had its share of independent operators. The Ideal fleet name was shared by the buses of R Taylor and H Wray, who jointly provided a service between Barnsley and Pontefract. In May 1961 Wray's BRN 263 is threading its way through a mass of Yorkshire Traction buses in Barnsley Bus Station to reach the stand for its next departure. It is a former Ribble 'White Lady', a Leyland PD1 with Burlingham bodywork, originally used on limited stop services across Lancashire. *Geoff Warnes*

The departure stands around Christ Church were served by five of Doncaster's leading independents, providing frequent all day services to the north-east of the town. Arguably the smartest of these fleets was that of Felix Motors, based in Hatfield. From 1953 until 1968, all fleet additions were new AECs; 34 was the second of these, a Regent III with synchromesh gearbox and handsome Roe bodywork, delivered in 1955. It is duplicating the service journey to Moorends, provided by bus 35 behind, the first of eight Regent Vs to join the fleet. Felix was the first of the Doncaster independents to succumb to the cheque book of the South Yorkshire PTE, selling out in April 1976. *Roger Holmes*

Sheffield

Sheffield's municipal public transport network was among the finest in the country – the tram system in particular was the envy of many other towns and cities. Much of this was due to the influence of A R Fearnley, general manager from 1904 to 1936. Trams still outnumbered buses in the fleet as late as 1948 yet, despite their suitability for Sheffield's hilly terrain, a decision to close the system was taken in 1951 – even before the last new cars had been delivered – and in October 1960 the city became the last in England to say farewell to its trams.

The bus network was extensive. Since 1929 it had been a complex operation, with three fleets under common management – one owned by the city, one by the railways (originally the LMS and LNER), and a third jointly owned by the city and the railways and run by a Joint Omnibus Committee ("JOC").

The network within the city boundaries was the largest and these (Category A) services were the responsibility of the city's Transport Department, as were the trams. The jointly-operated Category B services mainly ran into areas immediately beyond the municipal boundary in Derbyshire or the West Riding, creating complications when the city boundaries were later extended. Category C comprised a small group of longer-distance services to Bradford, Buxton, Chesterfield, Doncaster, Gainsborough, Huddersfield, Leeds and Manchester, almost all jointly run with other operators. Although there were separate fleets for each category, the three were managed as a whole, using the same garages and from the mid-1930s sharing a common image. Buses rarely moved between fleets on a permanent basis but pragmatic use of buses from the wrong fleet was a daily occurrence and some buses spent virtually all their time on the wrong category of service – administrative and financial adjustments took account of this. All this went largely unnoticed by the travelling public (as was the intention), and only the more observant would notice the subtle differences in fleetnames and legal lettering.

Sheffield's three fleets accounted for almost half the buses in South Yorkshire, with more than 800 in the early 1960s just after the replacement of the trams; a decade later this had dropped below 700 and around 680 passed to the South Yorkshire Passenger Transport Executive on 1 April 1974.

From 1930, double-deckers dominated, with AEC Regents and Leyland Titans the mainstay up to the 1960s, with over 500 of each. Wartime and early post-war pressures brought Guys, Daimlers and Crossleys but throughout the 1950s only AECs and Leylands were bought, including Atlanteans from 1959. Later, Daimler Fleetlines were added, becoming prominent after the last Regents arrived in 1964. The single-deck fleet was much smaller and until the end of the 1940s consisted almost entirely of AEC Regals and Leyland Tigers but later became more varied; from 1959 Leyland Leopard coaches were bought for use on rural and interurban services.

Sheffield's Central Bus Station occupied a large site between the railway station and the city centre, close to the busy markets area. The site was acquired in the 1930s but it was not until the 1950s that covered passenger accommodation was provided. Most bus operators serving the city used it – this May 1968 view shows four Sheffield buses waiting on Platform A with a Wigmore's single-decker at the front. Destinations and services were listed on both sides of the entrance to the covered waiting area for Platforms A and B. In the background are Midland Station, the flats at Norfolk Park and, on the right, Sheaf House. Opened in 1965, it displays the new logo launched that year when British Railways rebranded itself as British Rail. It was the railways' divisional headquarters. *Omnibus Society/ Roy Marshall*

The railway involvement meant partial state ownership of the JOC after nationalisation in 1948 and this later brought some unique vehicles to the B and C fleets, combining Leyland Leopard and Titan chassis with Eastern Coach Works bodywork – the latter then only available to the state-owned sector.

From the 1930s Sheffield's livery was light cream with azure blue relief, with many variations in their arrangement and, for many years, a thin red line below the lower-deck windows. In 1952 it was decided to change the livery to all-over green (for trams and buses). This proved highly unpopular and there was a very swift reversion to the previous colours. Cream and blue might have seemed impractical for an industrial city with relatively poor air quality but the Transport Department did its best to keep its buses clean and the livery survived to the end.

On abolition of the British Transport Commission in 1963 its holding in the JOC passed to the British Railways Board. In 1969 this was transferred to the newly-established National Bus Company and placed under the control of its subsidiary, Amalgamated Passenger Transport Ltd ('APT'). This proved the spur to rationalisation. Sheffield City Council bought APT's share of the B fleet and its associated operations, while the C fleet and its routes were divided between NBC (which took all but four of the 31-strong C fleet) and the Transport Department. From January 1970 the Department could run a simplified one-fleet operation but in little over four years the end came with the creation of the Metropolitan County of South Yorkshire.

During the 1930s AEC Regals and Leyland Tigers were bought in quantity and the fleet had a significant single-deck content. The last single-decker of pre-war specification was this 1939 Regal with Weymann body. Initially a demonstrator, it was acquired in 1940, becoming 54 in the B fleet. On withdrawal in 1955 it was converted into a mobile canteen and numbered M61 in the ancillary fleet. It was photographed at Castlegate. *Tom Robinson*

AEC and Leyland also supplied the majority of Sheffield's double-deckers during the decade, the sole exceptions being one bus each from Crossley and Daimler, which had both gone by 1937. By the early 1950s many of the survivors were careworn and 14 AEC Regents dating from 1938-40 were fitted with new bodywork by Roe in 1952/53. Three wartime Daimlers and a solitary Guy were similarly treated. In this form the Regents remained in service until 1960, latterly seeing little use. The oldest of the rebodied Regents was 356, pictured here at Pond Street on 28 August 1952 in the all-over green livery which was adopted and swiftly dropped during the space of a few months; in the face of a barrage of public criticism the blue and cream was reinstated.
C Carter/OnLine Transport Archive

After being allocated Daimlers and Guys during the war the Transport Department wanted to revert to its pre-war suppliers and as soon as it could placed orders with AEC and Leyland for more than 300 new buses. To supplement them 28 Crossleys were obtained between 1947 and 1949, most of which had originally been destined for other municipal fleets. The first to arrive, in mid-1947, were six SD42/3s with Crossley 32-seat bodywork ordered by Chesterfield Corporation. They were placed in the A fleet, numbered 237-242, yet spent much of their lives working JOC Peak District services. Three lasted until May 1962, outliving all the Regals and Tigers. 242 looks immaculate in this picture. Its service number aperture, displaying 40 for the Bakewell via Calver service, was a later addition to Chesterfield's single indicator box. *Tom Robinson*

Among the orders placed immediately after the end of the war was one for 100 AEC Regent chassis with 9.6-litre engines and pre-selector gearboxes. Weymann would have been the Transport Department's preferred bodybuilder for all of them but, despite an initial order for 55 bodies, they could only build 40. They were delivered for the A fleet in three distinct batches in 1947/48. The first ten – the first post-war specification buses to arrive – had straight side panels, whereas the next two batches, 15 each year, had Weymann's more usual outswept skirt panels as shown here on 1948 bus 257. It was photographed on 22 November 1962, towards the end of its life, leaving Bridge Street Bus Station on service 10. The grey roof was a feature of Sheffield buses from about 1948 until the early 1960s. *Malcolm King*

The first post-war single-deckers were Leyland PS1s delivered in 1947; by early 1949 36 were in service, spread across all three fleets, as well as three more powerful PS2s for the steeply-graded Stocksbridge local service introduced in 1948. They were rear-entrance 34-seaters and were to have had Weymann bodies. However, to overcome delivery delays two PS1s were instead bodied by Leeds-based Wilks & Meade (owned by coach operator Wallace Arnold), arriving in March 1948. B fleet 80 was one of the pair, distinguishable when new by its cream painted radiator. Another ten were bodied by T Cawood & Sons of Doncaster, a small coachbuilder which had previously undertaken rebuilding and overhaul work for the department.
Tom Robinson collection

Deliveries of Leylands resumed in 1947 when 21 Leyland-bodied PD2/1s joined the A fleet as 537-557. Some of them, number 545 included, put in very long service, lasting until 1966. In this early 1960s view the bus approaches the stop at Fulwood Church, inbound from Crimicar Lane to the city centre on service 60, with a backdrop of the Hallam Moors. The 'Motor Bus Fare Stage' stop flag is a real period piece, as is the Webb-patent sewer gas destructor lamp on the corner of Brookhouse Hill and Canterbury Avenue. *Martin Llewellyn*

Weymann bodied the other 24 PS1s and the three PS2s. C-fleet 1201 was one of the PS1s, delivered in 1948 as fleet number 201 and renumbered 1201 in 1953. Here it stands in Central Bus Station before operating category A service 31 to Hillsborough via Lower Walkley; this was introduced in 1954 and followed a short tortuous route through steep and narrow streets to the north-west of the city. It was single-deck operated despite the absence of any height restrictions and over the years saw many different vehicle types. In the background are a lowbridge AEC Regent III and a pair of Windover Kingsway coaches belonging to Sheffield United Tours, while in the distance, beyond the railway tracks, older buildings are about to be cleared from Park Hill. *Tom Robinson*

By early 1949 60 further PD2/1s with Leyland bodies had followed, including nine for the B fleet. Fleet numbering around this time seemed rather haphazard, with buses being allocated numbers freed up by withdrawn pre-war vehicles. Here 296, new in 1948, passes British Railways' Bridgehouses Goods Depot on the busy 151 from Shiregreen; having descended Chatham Street from Pitsmoor Road it will continue into Corporation Street to cross the River Don before reaching its final destination in Bridge Street. These too were long-lasting buses, and 296 survived until 1965, latterly with a cream roof; the photo was taken in January of that year and illustrates the growing fashion for continental cars, with a Citroën 2cv and a Volvo in view. *Graham Hague*

The A fleet had all but one of the 22 double-deck Crossleys. The first eight, delivered in late 1947, were DD42/5s with Crossley bodies, ordered by and built to the specification of Lancaster City Transport. The Crossleys were never as popular as the Leylands and AECs but, after upgrading with the "downdraught" engine, led full lives, being withdrawn between 1958 and 1962. One of their main haunts, particularly in their later years, was the Inner Circle, a nine-mile circuit around the city. Here one of the Lancaster buses, 574, stands outside Midland Station with a backdrop of Park Hill flats, its blinds set for an anti-clockwise run round the circle on service 8 (the clockwise equivalent was service 9). *Tom Robinson*

In the late 1940s bus operators and manufacturers alike were under great pressure and the fleet renewal programme underwent many changes as the Transport Department sought to achieve the earliest possible delivery dates. Available on short delivery, ten further Crossley DD42/5 chassis were ordered when it became clear that some of the AEC Regent chassis were to be delayed and the Crossleys were fitted with the Northern Coachbuilders bodies destined for the Regents. They included the solitary B fleet Crossley, fleet number 11, which was the first to go, in 1958. The rest were taken out of service in 1959/60 and converted into driver training vehicles, lasting in this role for several years in dark blue livery with grey roof. Four of the batch, including the former 593, 594 and 596, are in this line-up at the Central Bus Station. *Graham Hague*

The original plan for the 100 Regents was that Weymann would body 55, Northern Coachbuilders 30 and Cravens 15; in the event only 20 came from NCB and 40 from Weymann. Instead Charles Roberts & Co Ltd of Horbury, Wakefield, who were better known as builders of trams and railway wagons but also produced bus bodies, was able to meet the shortfall of 25. The A fleet received 15 during 1948, with the rest following soon afterwards for the B fleet. In August 1963 A-fleet 324 has just left Herries Road garage to take up service, by then mainly relegated to peak-hour extras such as service 94 from the estates in the north of the city to Templeborough. The last of the Roberts-bodied buses were withdrawn by the year end. *Malcolm King*

In 1948 twenty 7.7-litre engined AEC Regal Is were delivered, shared equally between the B and C fleets. They had standard Weymann bodies, similar to the PS1s. B fleet 112 was an example of a permanent transfer between the fleets – it was originally C fleet 196 (hence the registration). The change took place soon after delivery and resulted in the B fleet having eleven of the batch. It was photographed in the stacking area (the term used locally for parking buses between trips) adjacent to the Central Bus Station, with Joseph Rodgers & Sons' Sheaf Island Works in the background ('*The knife of kings, the king of knives*'). It had operated service 72 from Castleton. *Tom Robinson*

12

Sheffield's shortage of buses was made worse by the decision to abandon the Rotherham – Sheffield tram service, which the two corporations had operated jointly. It was temporarily split in December 1948 to allow reconstruction of the bridge over the canal and railway near Tinsley Station. It was then decided not to reinstate it, partly because of the poor state of Rotherham's tram fleet. To meet the need, four Crossleys originally ordered by Liverpool were obtained and entered service in January 1949 numbered 597-600. They had 4-bay Crossley bodies to Liverpool specification and 600 was photographed in the yard of East Bank Road garage beside an AEC Regent III with Roberts body. *Michael Eyre*

Among the 145 Leyland-bodied PD2/1s supplied between 1947 and 1949 were three (601-603) acquired from Leyland Motors' stock in 1949. Like the 'Liverpool' Crossleys, their purchase was prompted by the sudden closure of the Rotherham tram route. That they were not to Sheffield specification was evident from the non-standard one-piece indicator layout, half-drop windows and brown moquette seats. They also had constant-mesh gearboxes rather than the Sheffield's preferred synchromesh type. The tram-replacement 69 bus service – a category A operation as it ran entirely within the Rotherham and Sheffield municipal boundaries – was their usual duty, as shown here on 22 October 1963 by 603, heading towards Sheffield from Rotherham. This scene was soon to change drastically as the huge two-tier Tinsley viaduct was constructed to carry the new M1 motorway over the Don Valley, with a roundabout just behind the position of the bus. It opened in 1968. *Malcolm King*

Sheffield-based Cravens built many trams for the city up to 1927 and between 1933 and 1940 supplied almost 200 bus bodies on AEC Regal and Regent and Leyland Tiger, Titan and Titanic chassis. However Sheffield's only post-war double-deckers from the Darnall factory were 15 AEC Regent IIIs supplied in 1949/50, some of which lasted until 1967. Number 249 was photographed on 29 August 1963, descending Herries Road while working service 110 to Bridge Street from Parson Cross, a large council housing development north of the city. The Five Arches bridge in the background carried the electrified railway line from Sheffield Victoria to Manchester via Penistone and Woodhead. *Malcolm King*

The variety within the Sheffield fleets is nicely shown in this picture of the 'stacking' area adjacent to the Central Bus Station. Cravens-bodied AEC Regent 248 is nearest the camera, this and the picture above showing the strong similarity to the 120 RT-class Regents the firm built for London Transport in 1948/49 – even to the frame for the front indicators. Beyond are three Leyland-bodied PD2s, including 658 from the 1952 batch of PD2/10s (the last Leyland-bodied buses and the only new buses to enter service in the green livery), a Roe-bodied Regent III and a PD2 with Weymann bodywork. The application of the blue and cream livery is as varied as the buses themselves, with the two PD2s nearest the camera having the variant used for later Leyland bodies. *Graham Hague*

The protracted delivery of the 100 AEC Regents was completed in the winter of 1949/50 with the arrival of ten buses with Northern Coachbuilders bodies. They were the last of 40 bodies from the Newcastle upon Tyne firm (20 Regents, 10 Crossleys and 10 Daimler CVD6s – the latter the only post-war Daimlers in the fleet until the 1962 Fleetlines). 425 was in its final few months of service when photographed in July 1963, passing from Fargate into Pinstone Street and about to pass Sheffield Town Hall on the cross-city 24 service from Tinsley to Millhouses. *Martin Llewellyn*

After taking more than 70 half-cab single-deckers between 1947 and 1950 there was a desire to evaluate the new generation of underfloor-engined single-deckers and it was arranged for three of the new integrally-constructed Leyland-MCW Olympic model (built by Weymann) to be substituted for three of the PD2s that were on order. They arrived in early 1951 and were placed in the A fleet, although their initial use was mainly on longer-distance JOC services. The seating capacity of 44 was ten more than the Regals and Tigers, sufficient either to remove the need for a duplicate bus or replace a double-decker on a lightly used journey. A fourth Olympic joined them in 1953 after a spell as a demonstrator – the only used bus to join the fleet in the post-war period. Numbered 211, it is shown here in May 1968 (after being renumbered to 11 in 1967) as it passes Bridge Street Bus Station on single-deck operated service 31. It was withdrawn later in 1968. *Omnibus Society/Roy Marshall*

Named after their Wakefield-based maker, the 35 Roberts cars (502-536) were the ultimate in tramcar design in Sheffield and among the finest trams to run in this country. They were modelled on the Jubilee car 501 which was built in-house at Queens Road works in 1946. With the decision to close the city's tramway system being made in 1951, they were doomed from the start and their lives ridiculously short. Sheffield's trams never used service numbers, although in much earlier days route letters had been used. In this late 1950s view car 506 heads down High Street in the city centre, on its way to Vulcan Road at Tinsley, as 1957 Weymann-bodied AEC Regent 814 heads the other way, bound for Crookes on tram-replacement service 52. This was one of several cross-city bus services which maintained the same linkages as the trams had previously provided, although when buses took over the opportunity was taken to extend at each end of the route. Trams returned to this stretch of road in August 1994 as part of the new Supertram system. *Tom Robinson*

Opposite top The reduced order for 27 Titans emerged as a final 16 Leyland-bodied PD2/1s (delivered in 1951) and eleven PD2/12s. The latter were to the newly permitted dimensions of 27ft length and 8ft width and entered service in early 1952 with bodywork from two new suppliers. Two (361/362) came from Mann Egerton of Norwich, who were better known for single-deckers, coaches and bespoke car bodies and built only eight double-deckers. Originally 56-seaters (later increased to 58 and then 59), they had particularly well appointed interiors although their frontal appearance was slightly marred by the frame of the destination indicators. 361 is seen at Birley Rise, heading north from Hillsborough towards Fox Hill, on the indirect service 1 to the city centre via Firth Park and Attercliffe. *Malcolm King*

Opposite Roe bodywork appeared in the fleet when nine PD2/12s with Pullman style bodies featuring deep lower-deck windows entered service in January 1952. Leeds-based Roe continued to supply bodies to Sheffield until 1962 and all those on front-engined chassis initially carried the style of livery evolved for the later Leyland bodies. 387 is pictured heading towards the Moor from Pinstone Street in June 1964, working service 63. The batch was withdrawn and sold for scrap in 1968. *Martin Llewellyn*

17

Although 100 preselector-gearbox AEC Regent IIIs were in service by the end of 1950 the department wanted a synchromesh gearbox similar to the Leyland PD2s. Aware of the risk of losing Sheffield's business AEC agreed to supply nine more Regents with constant-mesh gearboxes and retro-fit Crossley-built synchromesh units that were shortly to become available. New in late 1952, they had four-bay Roe bodies. Numbered 18/19 and 113-119, in 1963 they became 2018/19, 2113-19 in the new B fleet series. 2114 is pictured in St Mary's Gate, Chesterfield, heading for East Midland's bus station at the end of a trip from Sheffield on service 64. This and the related 62 were created in 1961 by linking service 30 (Sheffield – Eckington) with East Midland's Eckington – Chesterfield service. Sheffield, Chesterfield Corporation and East Midland then shared their operation. *David Beilby*

After the Leyland Olympics the next underfloor-engined model to be tried was the AEC Regal IV; three arrived in March 1952 with Roe 44-seat bodies, numbered 212-214 in the A fleet. Unusually, they were initially owned by the chassis manufacturer's sales arm, ACV Sales, and were not bought until 1954; this perhaps explains the swoop on the front panels, uncharacteristic of the Sheffield fleet. Renumbered 12-14 in 1967 they were withdrawn a year later and number 12 was nearing the end of its career when photographed in Exchange Street awaiting a run on the infrequent service 58 to Thorpe Hesley. This had been started in 1932 by Arthur Kitson, whose coach company later became one of the key constituents of Sheffield United Tours, and was acquired in 1934. It was designated a Category B service, with Rotherham Corporation Transport taking a share in its operation from 1935. *Ken Jubb*

All new buses in 1953 were for the B fleet, which received its largest investment to date, necessary to keep pace with the expansion of services to new areas of housing. Among them were 26 Leyland PD2/12s with 58-seat Weymann bodywork. In August 1964, 2163 – as it had become the previous year – was parked in Harmer Lane, on the approach to Central Bus Station, after a journey from Bakewell on service 40. The small red W on the front dash panel denotes an 8ft-wide bus, at a time when many buses were still of the earlier 7ft 6in maximum width. *Ken Jubb*

Complementing the Leylands were ten AEC Regent IIIs with Roe bodies, this time fitted with synchromesh gearboxes from new. In January 1968 number 2177 is pictured opposite the long-gone Lansdowne Hotel at the start of London Road, heading for Batemoor on service 36, which involved the steep climb up Hutcliffe Wood Road to Abbey Lane. It has been repainted from its original livery with blue window surrounds into the standard style with three blue bands, while another indication of the slight livery variations introduced by Chaceley T Humpidge, who took over as General Manager in 1961, was the use of matt black paint between the separate blind apertures to create the impression of a single unit. *Martin Llewellyn*

Following the decision to abandon the tramways, the first of the major closures, on 27 March 1954, was the cross-city Middlewood to Ecclesall route. The replacement buses were 56 Weymann-bodied Leyland PD2/12s allocated, like all the tram-replacement buses, to the A fleet. Delivery started in late 1953. 721 stands at Fulwood Post Office before departing on an earlier tramway replacement service, the 88 via Nether Green and Hunters Bar to the city centre and on to Malin Bridge, which had only required 11 buses. *Graham Hague*

Two underfloor-engined single-deckers arrived in 1953 although it was 1955 before they entered service, mainly as a result of certification problems arising from their unconventional layout. They were Leyland Royal Tigers with Weymann bodies with an open rear platform of the style more usually found on double-deckers. They had 31 seats and an authorised standing capacity of 30 – intended to be comparable with a double-decker. Originally destined for service 54 to Rivelin and the 74 (Norton), neither of which seemed suited to this mode of operation, a change of plan saw them allocated to the 31 and they were rarely seen elsewhere. This picture of 222 shows the distinctive appearance as it descends Daniel Hill on its way to the city centre in August 1964. Half a century later the scene looked little different and remarkably the 31 was still running – operated by Optare Solos of Sheffield Community Transport. *Graham Hague*

For a period in the mid-1950s AEC won the bulk of Sheffield's orders. The last Regents with conventional bonnets and radiators were 36 with 58-seat Weymann bodywork delivered in 1954/55. B fleet 178 (2178 from 1963) was photographed passing the Millstone Inn on the long climb out of Hathersage towards Fox House and Sheffield on service 72 from Castleton. This was worked jointly with North Western, some of whose journeys extended beyond Castleton via Chapel-en-le-Frith to Manchester as service X72. North Western had a small depot in Castleton and only provided single-deckers for the 72 whereas the JOC introduced double-deckers during the 1950s in an effort to cater for the heavy demand over summer weekends – even so extensive duplication was still required. *Tom Robinson*

The 1954 Regents were shared by all three fleets, with 22 in the B fleet, 12 in the A fleet and two – the only ones with saloon heaters – in the C fleet. In October 1968 A-fleet 730 passes down Springfield Road in the more affluent south-western suburbs of the city, on the large clockwise loop of service 61; by contrast the terminus at Penrith Road in Shirecliffe was in an area of pre-war council housing north of the city centre which generated rather more bus passengers. By the time of the photograph, 730 was the last bus of the exposed-radiator style in Sheffield service; it was withdrawn at the end of the following month. *Martin Llewellyn*

Buses delivered after 1954 took on a new appearance as the Transport Department started to specify concealed radiators, which tended to emphasise the difference between the Regents and Titans. The first to arrive, in 1955, were 32 Roe-bodied AEC Regent IIIs for the B fleet. They had a distinctive appearance in their early years as illustrated by 1263, with the 'Roe livery', the blue surround to the AEC grille (which was of the style usually associated with the later Regent V model and unique to Sheffield on Regent IIIs), and the grey roof. After operating service 37 via Owler Bar and Baslow in June 1963, the bus has arrived at Rutland Square in Bakewell, where it is passing two rival grocery shops – Burgons and the larger one of local firm R Orme & Co. *Martin Llewellyn*

Lowbridge double-deckers played a minor role in the fleet; there had been a few in the early 1930s but the only post-war examples were nine 1956 AEC Regent IIIs with Weymann bodywork for the B fleet. They replaced an order for highbridge bodies from Roe, which instead went to the A fleet, Weymann agreeing to amend an order for 45 bodies to include nine lowbridge ones for the B fleet. They enabled double-deck operation of services 6 and 19 (Dinnington), 21 (Treeton) and 70 (Upton) which all negotiated low bridges. When the low height Bridgemasters took over the Dinnington services the need for side-gangway lowbridge buses was reduced and some of the Regents were sold in 1967, but 1286 was one of three that ran until 1970. In this May 1970 view at East Bank Garage it lacks the topmost blue band that these buses had carried when new, creating a livery variant unique to the lowbridge buses. *Martin Llewellyn*

45 PD2s with Weymann bodies were ordered for the April 1956 Intake to Walkley tram conversion. However, Leyland had ended production of its full synchromesh gearbox that the Transport Department considered essential for tram-replacement duties – the new gearbox only had synchromesh on 3rd and 4th. The order was cancelled and 45 AEC Regent IIIs ordered instead – the revised bonnet and radiator grille usually fitted to the Regent V again featured. In May 1968 Weymann-bodied 753 passes Bridge Street Bus Station on a football special. *Omnibus Society/Roy Marshall*

Forty AEC Regent Vs with Weymann bodies entered the A fleet in 1956/57 – the only short (27ft) Regent Vs in the fleet. Their primary function was to replace the Crookes to Handsworth tram service but they were widely used elsewhere, especially in later years. 794 is at the Norfolk Arms, which served as the Rivelin Dams terminus of service 54, requiring a reversing manoeuvre across the busy A57. Despite just entering Derbyshire this was a Category A service. Two JOC services continued beyond here; the 39 via the Snake Pass and Glossop to Manchester, and the 44 to Bamford and Bakewell – an extension of the original service to Derwent village, which was submerged beneath the waters of the Ladybower reservoir in 1943. *Graham Hague*

After a three-year absence more Leylands came in 1957, with 40 Roe-bodied PD2/20s for the A fleet and three for B fleet – the first PD2s for Sheffield with the Leyland full-width bonnet. 843 is pictured in its later years turning off the main road to Stocksbridge onto the private road into Ewden Valley, which, like Rivelin, was the location of reservoirs run by the corporation's waterworks department. Occasional service 81 journeys extended beyond Middlewood to reach Ewden, using the scenic road alongside More Hall reservoir for almost a mile. *Phil Drake*

When the railways were nationalised in 1948 the railway shareholding in the JOC passed to the British Transport Commission and this brought the opportunity to source bodywork from Eastern Coachworks, from then only available to state-owned operators. Thus, in 1957 the JOC fleets bought five Leyland PD2/20s with Eastern Coachworks bodies, similar to those fitted to later Bristol KSWs but looking very different with Leyland's full-width bonnet. Whether there was any advantage compared with the usual Roe or Weymann bodies is a moot point but the exercise was not repeated and the buses remained unique. 3152 was one of two allocated to the C fleet and was photographed in April 1969 entering Central Bus Station via Harmer Lane for a journey to Aston on service 85; a (very) short working of the Gainsborough service. The platform doors were a later addition, fitted in 1963. *Omnibus Society/Roy Marshall*

The B fleet had three of the ECW-bodied PD2s to the C fleet's two. In these photographs B fleet 1292 has just arrived at the picturesque Low Bradfield terminus of service 16, ready to return to the city. The turning manoeuvre involved the bus stopping outside the Cross Inn on Woodfall Lane, at the start of the formidable climb to High Bradfield, where it has confronted the Sunblest bakery van. It would then reverse round the corner to pick up the waiting passengers. Although barely four miles from Hillsborough the twin villages of High and Low Bradfield are within the Peak District National Park. *Graham Hague*

The final 41 Leyland PD2s for the A fleet came in late 1957 and early 1958, primarily to replace the Prince of Wales Road tram service. They had 59-seat bodywork from the usual suppliers of Weymann (20 buses) and Roe (21), all on PD2/30 chassis and in the different livery styles usually associated with the respective bodybuilders' products. Here two Weymann-bodied buses, 491 and 488, stand outside the Classic Cinema in Fitzalan Square in the city centre, both engaged on peak-hour extras. By the time of the photograph both buses have gained black surrounds to the blind apertures, while the Leyland badges fitted above the Midland Red style grilles have been carefully picked out in red to match the wheels. *Tom Robinson*

Sheffield's only AEC Reliance was this centre-entrance Roe Dalesman coach bought in 1958, mainly for use by the Transport Committee. Finished in all-over cream, for many years it ran without a fleet number — on paper it was numbered 900 until 1967 when it became 90. It was allocated to the A fleet but in later years saw use on rural bus services, particularly the 44 to Bakewell via Bamford. In this August 1969 picture it was arriving in Central Bus Station, probably to take up service. *Omnibus Society/Roy Marshall*

Throughout the 1950s all new Sheffield double-deckers had been either AEC Regents or Leyland Titans but December 1958 brought something different. The integrally-constructed AEC Bridgemaster with Park Royal bodywork was a way of overcoming the low bridge problem without resorting to the side-gangway layout; six were bought and placed in the A fleet, although all the services requiring low-height buses were in Categories B or C. They were the city's first 30ft-long double-deckers. In later years they were used on a range of duties and 520 is pictured drawing away from the cavernous passenger shelters on Pinstone Street, en route from Sheffield Lane Top to Bradway. *Graham Hague*

Between 1958 and 1960 the C fleet took another seven PD2s, fitted with Roe bodywork and platform doors for use on the longer interurban services. In April 1968 number 3156 (1156 until 1967, when the 3000-series was created for the C fleet) is shown pulling away from the stand in Doncaster's Southern Bus Station on service 77. This was the only service shared by the three South Yorkshire municipal operators, albeit in the case of Sheffield the Joint Omnibus Committee, although that did not preclude the regular appearance of A fleet buses. *Omnibus Society/ Roy Marshall*

Sheffield's first 30ft double-deckers from Leyland were 30 PD3/1s with Roe 69-seat bodies, delivered to the A fleet in 1959 with numbers 461-476 and 901-914. Half of them were bought to replace the Abbey Lane tram service, which was withdrawn at the end of February, while the balance were for modernising the bus fleet. When new they wore the usual livery for Roe bodies with blue window surrounds although by the time of this photograph 464 had been repainted into the standard three-band livery. It was pictured in May 1967 at the bottom of Corporation Street in Rotherham, ready to return to Sheffield via Tinsley on service 69. This service was always busy but on this occasion the queue was exceptional and the style of dress suggests a special occasion. A later order for more PD3s was amended to specify Atlanteans and the PD3s were the only ones of their type in the fleet – and the last of a very long line of Leyland Titans for the A fleet. *Ken Jubb*

Opposite top Sheffield was the only English city fleet to operate trams alongside the rear-engined double-deckers that started to make their mark at the end of the 1950s. During 1959, the last full year of tram operation, 25 Atlanteans were taken into stock; the first six were ordered for evaluation against the Bridgemasters, but before any trial could take place an order for more PD3s was switched to one for a further 19 Atlanteans. All 25 (363-368 and 881-899) had 78-seat Metro-Cammell bodies. The larger batch was used to replace the Wadsley Bridge to Woodseats trams from 3 October 1959 but when pictured in Ivy Park Road, Crosspool, 894 was in use on the anti-clockwise Outer Circle (service 2), a circuit of the city that took almost two hours to complete. It traversed some higher ground, particularly in the Crosspool area, which was often affected by snow as in this January 1963 scene. *Martin Llewellyn*

Opposite Until 1959 the three fleets had only 15 underfloor-engined single-deckers: an AEC Reliance, two Leyland Royal Tigers, three AEC Regal IVs, four Leyland Olympics and five AEC-Park Royal Monocoaches (delivered in 1955 and of which there is no colour picture available). None really suited Sheffield's requirements. When the half-cab single-deckers needed replacing, Leyland was preparing to launch the powerful O.600-engined Leopard and that did suit – Sheffield's first were specials supplied before the Leopard was announced. The first six, in 1959, had Weymann Fanfare coach bodies – an unusual choice for bus service use – and were intended for the longer JOC services. Eight more followed in 1960/61. In May 1970 number 1002, which had been moved from the C to the B fleet in 1967 and renumbered from 1302, was on the Stocksbridge local service 257, which ran entirely outside the city boundary – the number hints at its role as a feeder to service 57 to Sheffield. Here at Station Road, Deepcar, it has met Baddeley Brothers' former Halifax JOC Albion Nimbus on their service from Holmfirth. *Ian Wild*

The 30ft AEC Regent appeared in the fleet in 1960 when 71 were delivered, all 2D3RA models. Among them were 25 for the B fleet (1325-1349) with 69-seat Roe bodywork and platform doors for use on JOC services. They were the last Sheffield buses with Roe's teak-framed body and when new were in the style of livery applied to Roe bodies. In later days 1335, repainted into standard livery, was photographed passing the impressive Abbeydale Cinema. *Graham Hague*

The A fleet took 46 Regent Vs for the penultimate stage of the tram replacement programme, which involved the Meadowhead to Sheffield Lane Top service. They were delivered in early 1960, allowing the conversion to take place in early April. 447 was one of 26 (435-460) with Weymann 69-seat bodies, and was photographed looking rather past its prime against a backdrop of dense terraced housing in Petre Street, which had been served by trams until the first route closure way back in 1925. Service 34 was a cross-city route from the southern suburbs to Grimsethorpe, with its terminus at the Wesleyan Reform Chapel on Upwell Street. *Tom Robinson*

For the April 1960 tram conversion there were also 20 AEC Regents with Alexander bodies (861-880). Readily identifiable by their prominent front domes, they were Sheffield's first buses from the Scottish manufacturer. All the A fleet Regents of 1960 had open rear platforms but these were the last and the relatively small number of front-engined buses which followed had forward entrances. 879 is pictured on the long steep climb up East Bank Road in September 1963. Service 43 was introduced to cater for the substantial 1960s housing developments in the Gleadless Valley and was placed jointly in Categories A and B, giving the corporation a 75% share. *Martin Llewellyn*

Most of the 84 first-generation Leyland Atlanteans received between 1959 and 1963 had Metro-Cammell or Weymann bodies but six had Roe bodies and 1960 bus 369 was unique in having Alexander bodywork, with the same prominent front dome as the Regent Vs. It is seen here on Penistone Road, shortly before turning left to cross the River Don via Hillfoot Bridge to reach the city centre via Neepsend Lane. It is working service 42, one of those introduced in 1959 to replace the Wadsley Bridge to Woodseats trams, by now extended to run from Fox Hill to Low Edges, an area of housing in the far south of the city adjacent to the Derbyshire boundary. Few Sheffield Atlanteans had Leyland badges on the front – 369 was one. *Graham Hague*

A new supplier, Burlingham, provided nine 41-seat dual-purpose bodies on Leyland Leopard chassis in 1960 (the one in this picture is wrongly badged as a Tiger Cub). They had one-piece coach-style doors and replaced half-cab single-deckers on JOC services – four going to the B fleet and five to the C fleet. In September 1960 C-fleet 1179 was photographed beside a typical Sheffield-design bus stop on the approach to Exchange Station, Manchester, then the terminus of service 48. Being across the River Irwell, the stop – which is completely lacking in passenger facilities – was actually situated in Salford, not Manchester. These vehicles were later converted for one-man operation with folding doors, rather spoiling their appearance, and in 1967 this bus was renumbered to become 3079 in the new C fleet series. *Geoffrey Morant*

The A fleet took five Leopards with 44-seat Weymann bodies in 1960. One was number 7 (renumbered from 207 in 1967), seen here at Load Brook, surely Sheffield's remotest terminus. In 1966 it was one of the first two buses converted for one-man operation although it was 1967 before this mode of operation was introduced. Service 117 operated twice a week, on Saturday afternoons, and this June 1967 image shows the later journey which left the outer terminus at 5.45pm. The bus has already reversed at the junction with Long Lane to return via Beeton Green, Load Brook, Storrs, Stannington and Hillsborough to the city centre. Despite the isolated location, the Transport Department had installed a stop sign ('Motor bus leaves here for Sheffield') and timetable case. One wonders how often anyone boarded a bus at this isolated spot. *Ian Wild*

More unique ECW-bodied Leylands were received in 1961, this time five Leopard L1s with the style of bodywork normally found on Bristol chassis. As with the Leopards with Weymann Fanfare and Burlingham bodies they were shared between the B and C fleets; the three C fleet vehicles included 3082 (1182 until 1967), shown here in Halifax on 8 September 1968. Sheffield buses reached Halifax only in April of that year when the long-standing service 68 from Sheffield to Huddersfield via Penistone was extended northwards. Previously a joint operation with Yorkshire Traction, under the new service pattern alternate journeys became the limited-stop X68 and the Halifax and Huddersfield JOCs started to participate in the operation. *John Kaye*

The variety in the single-deck fleet increased further when four Leopards with Park Royal 45-seat bodies arrived for the B fleet in 1961. Number 12 (originally 1316 and then 1016 from 1967 to 1970) is seen at Douglas Road, Parkwood Springs, in February 1974 with the later *sans-serif* style fleetname. It was operating the infrequent and short-lived service 100 introduced in 1970 to link this isolated community with the city centre, which was little over a mile away. Parkwood Springs was built in the mid-19th century to house railway employees working at the nearby Neepsend engine shed; by the early 1970s the housing was reaching the end of its life and what remained was soon to be demolished. The destination may never have been added to destination blinds. *Barry Ridge*

Fleet number 525 was Sheffield's only forward-entrance AEC Bridgemaster, with a 72-seat body by Park Royal. It arrived in 1961 following the earlier delivery of six rear-entrance versions and was the only double-decker acquired that year. Like the other Bridgemasters it was placed in the A fleet although here it is working the 45, a Category B service. On 16 April 1967 the bus has stopped to drop passengers off at the start of Abbeydale Road South, close to the junction with Archer Road and Springfield Road. *Martin Llewellyn*

The 24 Weymann-bodied Leyland Atlanteans of 1962 were spread across all three fleets – the smallest allocation was to the C fleet, which only had three. On 7 March 1970, during its final days in Sheffield and by now in the merged fleet, former C fleet 3163 was photographed in the Millhouses turning circle, which had previously been used by the trams. In later years it became the terminus of service 24 which ran across the city to Tinsley (Highgate), close to the municipal boundary with Rotherham. After the demise of the JOC in 1970, the three Atlanteans together with the remaining C-fleet Titans all passed to Yorkshire Woollen District for further use in West Yorkshire. The conductress, wearing white boots, is returning to the bus from the row of shops behind. *Martin Llewellyn*

The A fleet also received six Roe-bodied Atlanteans in 1962; they had none of the style of earlier Roe bodies in the fleet and were turned out in standard livery. The ungainly bodywork incorporated framing supplied by Park Royal and had particularly shallow upper-deck windows. On a gloomy day, with the Odeon Cinema towering above it, 949 stands on Flat Street, the city terminus of the frequent service 71. *Graham Hague*

Dual-sourcing mattered to Sheffield so, with AEC showing no sign of developing a rear-engined model, long-standing manager R C Moore placed an order for three Daimler Fleetlines in early 1961. They were among the first Fleetlines produced and joined the A fleet in 1962 along with a dozen Atlanteans with similar Weymann 77-seat bodies. They were the first Daimlers since 1948 and the first Gardner-engined buses since the wartime Guys (the last of which was withdrawn in the year the Fleetlines came). 952 is at the Flat Street departure point for service 71 in March 1973. *Martin Llewellyn*

General manager R C Moore retired in 1961, having been in charge since 1945. His replacement was Chaceley T Humpidge, previously general manager at Bradford, which had a fleet of 30ft-long forward-entrance AEC Regent Vs. He ordered 31 similar buses for 1963/64 delivery, with 70-seat bodywork by Park Royal or Weymann. After three years of buying rear-engined double-deckers traffic manager Philip Baggaley had wanted more of the latter and maybe his view prevailed as there were no more AEC double-deckers after 1964 and no more with front engines. The ten Weymann buses were for the A fleet and arrived in 1963, numbered 64-73 instead of the intended 964-973. They were twice renumbered and the former 64 (by then 1384) is shown on Montgomery Road in May 1972 bound for the terminus of service 97 at Nether Edge Hospital. *Martin Llewellyn*

Apart from the forward-entrance Bridgemaster the forward-entrance Regent Vs were Sheffield's only buses of this configuration. Of the Park Royal buses 19 joined the B fleet while the C fleet had two. 1368, a 1964 bus, was photographed in June 1967 at the Nethergate terminus of service 7 in Stannington, high above Hillsborough between the Loxley and Rivelin valleys. The first service to Stannington, then an isolated village, was initiated by Henry Thrale, who sold his bus operations to the JOC in 1932; it was only in 1951 that service 7 was extended beyond Malin Bridge to the city centre. The cows confirm that suburban life had not entirely taken over. *Ian Wild*

The Daimler Fleetlines of 1962 were considered a success and another 55 followed in 1964/65. They were allocated to the A fleet and had distinctive Park Royal bodywork which broke away from the box-like shape of previous rear-engined double-deckers. New in 1965, 107 is pictured on Crimicar Lane at Fulwood, bound for the city centre on service 60, which was unique in terminating right outside Midland Station rather than using Central Bus Station. *Graham Hague*

The same style of Park Royal bodywork featured on 58 PDR1/2 Atlanteans, which used the Fleetline type of rear axle to achieve a lower overall height. Delivered in 1966 and initially placed in the A fleet, twelve moved to the B fleet within a few months. In May 1968, 141 was at Bridge Street, heading north to High Green on service 80. This was one of several services to this sector of the city that used the slightly out-of-the-way Bridge Street Bus Station rather than the Central Bus Station, while a few others terminated in streets on the fringes of the city centre instead of using either bus station. 1968 saw the delivery of some similar-looking buses but to full-height specification. *Omnibus Society/Roy Marshall*

Bus body building returned to Sheffield in 1964 when Neepsend Coachworks was set up by the John Brown group, which had acquired the Cravens business and also owned East Lancashire Coach Builders of Blackburn. Local politics ensured that Sheffield was an early customer and 20 bodies were ordered for Leyland PDR1/2 chassis The buses went into the A fleet as 341-360 in 1964/65, with 20 more (162-181) following in 1966. Built at the new factory in Neepsend Lane, the bodies were to an East Lancs design. The Neepsend venture was not a great success and bus body production ended in 1968. In August 1967 and looking smart without advertising, 173 passes down the Moor on its way to Fulwood on service 88. *Geoffrey Morant*

A unique bus added to the A fleet in 1966 was this Bedford VAS1 with 22-seat Cravens body, understood to have been built at the Darnall factory despite the opening of the new plant at Neepsend. It was bought for use by the Transport Committee, replacing the much more sumptuous Roe Dalesman coach. Like its predecessor it saw some use on bus services. Originally numbered 11, it was renumbered 1 in 1967, and was photographed in March 1972 in Central Bus Station displaying service number 190 for a peak-hour operation between Darnall and Firth Park. A TIM ticket machine is mounted beside the driver, although at some stage the bus was regularly used without a conductor on service 44 to Bakewell with a hand-held ticket machine. It was withdrawn and sold in 1973. *Omnibus Society/Peter Henson*

Like many other cities Sheffield turned to rear-engined single-deckers in the late 1960s, with a view to widespread one-man-operation. The initial order was for 33 AEC Swifts with Park Royal bodies, which arrived in 1968; 22 were dual-doorway 49-seaters for the A fleet. However, double-deck one-man-operation was now legalised and early trials confirmed that this was the way forward. As a result ten Swifts were offered for sale when they were just three years old but only four found a buyer, going to Hardwick's Services of Scarborough. A use was found for some of the remaining dual-door Swifts when the City Clipper service started on 13 December 1971, linking the bus and railway stations, other central terminal points and the city's main shopping areas. It conveniently required six buses and proved popular, later becoming the home of the UK's first articulated buses in PTE days. 17 is pictured at the stop in Angel Street, with another following. *John Hardey*

The other eleven Swifts of 1968 had 53-seat single-door bodies and were allocated to the B fleet as 1019-1029. They were later renumbered to become 39-49 and were then joined in 1970 by five more single-door Swifts (50-54), this time 50-seaters. In this March 1970 picture with its background of limestone walls typical of the Peak District, 39 passes through Hassop, on its way to Bakewell. *Omnibus Society/Peter Henson*

The easternmost extremity of the Sheffield network was in Gainsborough, almost half way to the east coast, and well over 60 miles from its western limit in Manchester. Here A-fleet Swift 22 stands at the terminus in Lord Street, Gainsborough. The journey back to Sheffield by way of Retford and Worksop was scheduled to take around 2 hours 20 minutes. In earlier years double-deckers were regularly used on the Sheffield to Retford section but Retford to Gainsborough had to be single-deck operated, requiring passengers to change buses in Retford – for this reason a bus was outstationed at Retford for many years. *Michael Fowler*

A new standard bus started to appear in the fleet in late 1968, combining the 33ft-long Leyland Atlantean PDR2/1 chassis with stylish 79-seat dual-doorway Park Royal bodywork. By the end of 1970 there were 163 in service – they transformed the fleet and became the most numerous type ever operated. Crucially, they allowed the widespread adoption of one-man double-deck operation. When the B fleet was absorbed, the modern image was further emphasised by a change of fleetname style, to 'Sheffield transport', using lower case lettering except for the initial S. In this June 1972 picture 731 (originally B fleet 1131) is passing the newly opened Sheaf Valley Swimming Baths. The substantial steel bumper bar was a feature of most Sheffield buses from 1967. *Ken Jubb collection*

After the first 68 buses, the design was altered to provide a raised driving position. This necessitated a deeper windscreen, which in turn required a revised arrangement for the destination indicators; there was also a tidier design of front panel. This picture of Leyland Atlanteans loading for a football match at Owlerton shows 572 with the new version, followed by one of the previous type with the shallower windscreen. Whitbread's Exchange Brewery is on the left of the picture. *John Hardey*

In 1968 four 49-seat Leyland Leopards were received for use on category C services. Another six followed in 1970, entering the merged fleet after the end of JOC operations. They all had Alexander Y-type bodies, ideally suited for longer stage-carriage services, and became the mainstay of Sheffield's contribution to the White Rose Express services X31-X34, which were introduced on 18 October 1969 and took advantage of the M1 motorway extension to provide fast links from Sheffield to Bradford, Halifax, Leeds and selected intermediate points. Number 56 was one of those delivered in 1970 and in this April 1972 picture has just left Leeds Central Bus Station for a non-stop journey to Sheffield. The high-speed run was scheduled to take 55 minutes. *Geoffrey Morant*

After eight years at the helm general manager Chaceley Humpidge retired in April 1969 and his replacement was Noel MacDonald, previously general manager at Coventry City Transport. The new appointment, coupled with some dissatisfaction with recent Atlanteans, led to Daimler Fleetlines returning to favour and all 48 buses delivered in 1971 were of this model. They had Park Royal bodywork of similar design to the Atlanteans. Eighteen were 30ft-long 76-seater single-door and the other 30 were 33ft-long 79-seater dual-door.

Above: One of the 30ft Fleetlines, 244, photographed in April in the Central Bus Station soon after entering service ready for a one-man operated journey on service 22. *Below:* Also photographed when new, 33ft dual-door Fleetline 700 in June 1971. *Omnibus Society/Peter Henson*

Another 20 Fleetlines arrived in 1972, this time with Alexander bodies – the first double-deckers from the Scottish manufacturer since 1960. They reverted to the rounded style of front and rear dome, rather than the peaked style featured on the Park Royal bodies supplied from 1968 onwards. Having just left Central Bus Station, 260 was photographed in Sheaf Street in March 1973, with a backdrop of Park Hill flats. The Access advert alongside heralds the arrival of the credit card era. *Omnibus Society/Roy Marshall*

Doncaster and Rotherham Corporations both had a long association with Bristols but neither came back for more when they returned to the market in the late 1960s. In contrast, Sheffield had no Bristols until 1972 when 18 Gardner-engined VRs with East Lancs bodies were bought – replacing a cancelled order for 25 Bristol RELL6Ls with Seddon dual-door bodies. The VRs compared unfavourably with the Atlanteans and were usually used on less arduous services such as the relatively flat 57 to Stocksbridge, where 278 is pictured passing the steelworks in October 1972. At the time the 57 served the floor of the Upper Don Valley with connecting single-deck operated local services providing the links to the estates up on the valley sides. The VR's front radiator access prohibited the fitting of the usual front bumper. *Omnibus Society/Peter Henson*

In 1973 Daimler Fleetlines and Leyland Atlanteans joined the fleet. The Atlanteans were of the improved AN68 model and included 22 with single-door Alexander bodywork. Photographed after the PTE took over (as evidenced by the 2-prefix to the service number), 305 stands at Calver Sough on the service to Bakewell via Grindleford. Behind it is a former member of the Sheffield fleet, the one-time number 10, a Weymann-bodied Leopard L1 running for Hulleys of Baslow. *Graham Hague*

Also delivered in 1973 were 14 Atlanteans with East Lancs bodies of similar design to those of the Bristol VRs. In this May 1973 picture, 313 was one-man operated on the clockwise Woodhouse circular, service 32. Behind it on Platform B of the Central Bus Station was Alexander-bodied 297; both had only recently been placed in service. *Omnibus Society/Peter Henson*

The final buses to enter service with Sheffield before the PTE took over were 30 Park Royal-bodied Daimler Fleetlines delivered in autumn 1973. They were of the shorter length but had dual-doors, previously only fitted to 33ft-long buses. In August 1973 779 was photographed at the Midland Station terminus of service 60. Buses on this service were fitted with the Videmat self service ticket machine, which was being trialled by several large operators. *Omnibus Society/Peter Henson*

The buses and the stop at Midland Station carried signs showing which side of the entrance to use, giving the option of driver service or the self service Videmat for passengers with the right change as an alternative to paying the driver. Self-service passengers boarded through the right-hand side of the entrance door, put coins into the machine to pay the fare and the Videmat issued a ticket printed with an image of the coins. Both buses are 33ft Fleetlines from the 1971 batch. *John Hardey*

Doncaster

The establishment of the Great Northern Railway's main works in Doncaster in 1853 was a catalyst for the rapid growth of the town. By the 1880s, horse bus services were being provided by several private operators. In 1898 the Council decided to establish its own electric tramways and services commenced in 1902: firstly to Balby and Hexthorpe on 2 June, and to the Race Course later in the same month. A service to Bentley commenced in the same year – this lay north of the GNR rail crossing and was isolated from the main system until a bridge over the railway was completed in 1911. Several more tram services followed, the final new route opening in 1916. This ran to Brodsworth, partly on reserved track alongside the Great North Road. In 1920 the Council appointed its first Transport Manager, Mr T Potts, who would remain in office until 1953 – prior to this, the tramway system had been run by the Electricity Committee. One of his first concerns was the growth of pirate motor bus operators whose services were running alongside the Corporation's trams. Many of these originated in the mining communities that were springing up outside the town with the development of deep coal mining. Accordingly in 1921 Doncaster applied for, and gained powers to run motor bus services to a number of these communities. The first (to Skellow, Rossington and Hatfield) commenced in 1922. Further routes followed in the next decade.

Much of the tramway was single-track with passing loops which dictated the frequency at which cars could operate. Consideration was given to replacing the trams with motor buses but the attraction of using the Corporation's own electricity was partly responsible for the decision to replace the tram network with trolleybuses (with the exception of the long route to Brodsworth).

Trolleybus services commenced in 1928, with four Garretts and six Karriers; the three-axle Karrier E6 with Roe bodywork becoming the standard choice for trolleybus deliveries, apart from one of the two trolleybuses built by Bristol which was acquired in 1932. By contrast, the motor bus fleet was very varied with Bristol, Dennis, Karrier, Daimler, Leyland and AEC – the last two supplying both two and three axle chassis. By the end of 1942 the only new vehicles available were to the Ministry of Supply's utility specification and nine Karrier 4-wheelers with utility bodywork, plus a number of utility motor buses joined the fleet. Early post-war deliveries continued the variety, with double-deckers from Daimler, Bristol and Leyland, before relative standardisation with a batch of 20 Roe-bodied Daimler CVD6s delivered in 1948-9.

Mr Potts then ordered three trial 8ft-wide vehicles, two double-deckers, on Daimler CVD6 and AEC Regent III chassis respectively, plus an underfloor-engined AEC Regal IV single-decker with a centre entrance, all with Roe bodies. The 8ft-wide buses proved a problem in the congested streets of 1950s Doncaster; the two double-deckers were sold to local operators in 1955 and the single-decker never found a truly useful role in the undertaking. The trial did however lead to a decision to standardise on AEC chassis with Roe bodies. Twelve 7ft 6in-wide Regent IIIs were ordered, plus three 30-foot long Regal IIIs, the latter for use on the joint service to Sheffield. These arrived in 1953, following delivery of two Leyland PD2s. In the meantime the trolleybus fleet was updated with the acquisition of six 1949 BUT two-axle trolleybuses with East Lancashire bodywork from Darlington Corporation.

General Manager Potts retired in 1953 and was replaced by Tom Bamford, who favoured two-axle vehicles for the trolleybus fleet. A scheme was drawn up to modernise the wartime Karrier W vehicles with new Roe 62-seat bodies. In 1954 the opportunity was taken to purchase nine more similar vehicles from Southend-on-Sea which were placed in service in original condition, with a view to rebodying as soon as practicable. Subsequently further chassis were acquired from the Mexborough & Swinton Traction Co and Pontypridd Urban District Council; all were fitted with new bodywork. In all, a fleet of 28 similar Karrier or Sunbeam Ws (an early example of badge engineering – both models were identical) with modern Roe bodywork was accumulated, replacing the remaining pre-war 6-wheelers and the former Darlington BUTs. Tom Bamford soon gained a reputation for tight cost control, which was to shape the undertaking for the 18 years he was in charge. He adopted the lightweight AEC Regent V with 7.7-litre engine, synchromesh gearbox, exposed radiator and Roe bodywork as the double-deck standard, 31 being obtained between 1955 and 1960.

The future of the trackless network had seemed assured, despite the abandonment of the Bentley service in 1956 due to extensive disruption during the replacement of the Mill Bridge over the River Don, but by 1961 the tide had turned and trolleybus abandonment was begun

Doncaster's fleet additions during the 1930s included buses from a variety of manufacturers including AEC, Leyland, Dennis, Daimler and Bristol. Single-deck deliveries in 1939 consisted of a batch of four Bristol L5Gs with Roe bodywork, numbered 14-17. Still in original condition on 10 March 1956, 14 is in the small North Bridge Bus Station for a trip to Skellow. This bus station, a large lay-by on stilts attached to North Bridge, which carried the Great North Road over the East Coast main railway line, was built to provide a turning facility necessary when trolleybuses replaced trams on the Bentley service. Bus 14 had a long life. In 1956, it was transferred to the Education Dept. Allocated letter A and painted green and white, it carried children to school and to swimming baths until the end of 1961. It was then rebuilt for the carriage of handicapped people and transferred to the Civic Welfare Dept. It finally left Council ownership in 1965 when 26 years old. *Geoff Warnes*

in earnest. The first conversions utilised a batch of one-man operated AEC Reliances. For the remaining conversions, it was decided to transfer the 20 newest trolleybus bodies on to new and used diesel bus chassis. The last trolleybus ran in December 1963. In the meantime the motor bus fleet was being updated with double-deck deliveries split between Leyland and Daimler, whilst unique batches of Leyland Royal Tiger Cubs allowed for expansion of one-man operation in the town. Batches of Seddon RUs and Daimler Fleetlines followed.

By the time Tom Bamford retired, Doncaster had the lowest municipal fares in the country, yet still remaining profitable. His place was taken by Robert Davies, who set about updating the department's image. A revised livery, with a startling purple stripe, outlined in white, was designed by students at the town's art college. But the end was nigh, as on 1 April 1974 the undertaking was swallowed up on the formation of the South Yorkshire Passenger Transport Executive.

In 1941 Doncaster was allocated three new Bristol L5Gs which had been intended for Bristol Tramways' own fleet. These had bodywork built in Bristol's Body Building Works in Brislington. In 1957, when one might have expected them to have reached the end of their useful lives, all three were converted for one man operation, primarily for use on Doncaster's small number of infrequent more lightly used services. Apart from an angled nearside front window and driver-operated door, the buses remained remarkably original until the end of 1961 when a batch of new AEC Reliances arrived. Number 20 was then retained for use as a driver trainer, and had three-inch wide strips of timber attached to each side to bring the overall width up to 8 feet. In this form it helped to retrain the Corporation's trolleybus drivers for motor bus operation. *Geoffrey Morant*

Doncaster commenced trolleybus operation in 1928, soon converting all of the tramway services (except the Brodsworth service, which continued with trams until motor buses took over in 1935). It soon standardised on the Karrier E6 six-wheeler with bodywork by Roe and 359 (originally numbered 59) is one of 20 similar vehicles which entered service in 1939. On 18 September 1955 it is standing at the town terminus of the service to Balby, the busiest service on the network. Some distance behind 359 can be seen a tubular steel barrier where a few intending passengers await arrival of the Hexthorpe trolleybus. *Geoff Warnes*

In 1954 Doncaster took the opportunity to purchase nine trolleybuses from Southend Corporation. These were Sunbeam W with semi-utility bodywork by Brush (384) or Park Royal (385 – 392), dating from 1945/6. The Sunbeam W chassis was identical to the Karrier W already in the fleet, both marques being in the ownership of the Rootes Group at the time of manufacture. Trolleybus 384 is pictured on Thorne Road en-route to Wheatley Hills on 18 June 1955. The Beckett Road and Wheatley Hills services followed the same route out of the town centre, sharing several of the same stops, and the destination blinds for Wheatley Hills had red lettering to assist passengers in distinguishing between the two services. 384 would be fitted with a new Roe body in 1959 and following withdrawal in 1961 this bodywork was transferred to new Daimler CVG6 motor bus 169.

Geoff Warnes

Having been allocated nine Karrier 4-wheelers with utility bodies during World War 2, Doncaster looked to modernise its trolleybus fleet with more four-wheelers. In 1952 an opportunity arose to purchase six 1949 BUT 9611T trolleys with East Lancashire bodies from Darlington Corporation. These were often to be seen on the Bentley route and on 20 August 1955 381 has just completed the long one-way loop around the New Village and is turning from Askern Road into Bentley High Street to return to Doncaster. At this time service numbers were often ignored – the Bentley route was actually service 1. Albion Valkyrie DYG 53 of South Yorkshire Motors is passing in the other direction, almost certainly on that operator's hourly service from Doncaster to Pontefract via Askern and Knottingley. *Geoff Warnes*

Trolleybus 383 was numerically the last of the former Darlington BUTs. On 23 August 1956 it was operating on the Hexthorpe route and has just passed the point where the Hexthorpe overhead parted from that of the Balby service and is just about to cross St James's Bridge over the East Coast main railway line. Behind the trolleybus, the tower of the YMCA building marks the junction of St Sepulchre Gate and Cleveland Street. By this time, 383 had received the brighter but simpler livery of crimson lake with one cream band, without lining out. In 1959 the six former Darlington BUTs were withdrawn and sold to Bradford, where all bar one entered service with their third operator, having been fitted with new bodywork. *Geoff Warnes*

At the end of 1954, Doncaster set about modernising its trolleybus fleet. The Karrier W chassis were sound but the wartime bodywork was beyond economic repair and they were fitted with new 62-seat Roe bodies. Further used chassis were acquired from Mexborough & Swinton and from Pontypridd UDC, all of which were rebodied by Roe before entering service. The former Southend vehicles received similar treatment and by the end of 1959 the Corporation had a fleet of 28 similar trolleybuses with modern bodywork. Several years after receiving its new body, 372 is seen turning out of Broxholme Lane at the point where the Beckett Road and Wheatley Hills routes converge. Twenty of the new Roe bodies would be transferred to motor bus chassis during the trolleybus abandonment programme but that on 372 was not one of them and it went for scrap after withdrawal in October 1963. Strangely, several of the native Karriers including 372 above were fitted with "Sunbeam" badges on rebodying. *Fred Ivey*

The final trolleybuses to enter service in Doncaster were a pair of 1947 Sunbeam Ws acquired as bare chassis from Mexborough & Swinton in 1957 and fitted with the customary new Roe bodywork before entry into service. The second of the pair, 354 is travelling along High Street where a new MacFisheries shop is being fitted out. A Thames Trader truck of Yorkshire Egg Producers is delivering to a nearby shop. 354 would run in this form until October 1963 and was then the last trolleybus to have its body transferred to a motor bus chassis. It re-entered service in 1964 fitted to the chassis of 1951 Leyland PD2/1 123, the Leyland body of which had been removed for scrap. *Omnibus Society/Roy Marshall*

During the late 1950s, buses to Highfields and Woodlands departed from a temporary bus station off Trafford Street. This view, dating from 7 May 1959 features 57, a 1941 AEC Regent with 8.8 litre engine and Roe bodywork, built to full pre-war standards. It would serve the Corporation for a full 20 years before withdrawal in 1961. Behind, Leyland-bodied PD2/1 number 95 is waiting to depart for Woodlands whilst alongside, Weymann bodied Daimler CWA6 87 has just arrived from Highfields. In 1963, the chassis of Leyland 95 would be fitted with the 1955 Roe body from trolleybus 397 and it would run in this form until withdrawal from service in August 1973. Daimler 87 would be withdrawn later in 1959.
Geoff Warnes

Another bus which had a long life with Doncaster was 60, seen crossing Balby Bridge on a trip to Edlington in August 1959. It was supplied in 1942 under the Ministry of Supply's unfrozen scheme which, following a freeze on the construction of new buses, allowed manufacturers' stocks of parts to be built up into complete buses. 60 had an AEC Regent chassis with 7.7 litre engine and crash gearbox, and Roe bodywork, the framework of which utilised pre-war stocks of teak, finished off to so-called utility standard. It would complete 20 years of useful service for Doncaster before withdrawal in 1962.
Geoff Warnes

The service to Edlington was nominally jointly operated with East Midland Motor Services, though in practice East Midland buses did not operate on the route. Low railway bridges on Edlington Lane meant that the service could only be operated by single-deckers, or side gangway lowbridge double-deckers. Doncaster's first lowbridge double-deckers were three Guy Arab IIs (84-86) with Gardner 5LW engines and Roe utility bodies, originally fitted with wooden seats and new in 1943. On 10 March 1956, number 85 stands in Glasgow Paddocks Bus Station in the maroon livery with three cream bands and full lining out. It had been withdrawn along with number 84 in 1954 and sent to Tiger Coaches (dealers) in Salsburgh, Scotland, but was soon recalled when an accident disabled 86. 85 was rebuilt by Roe before re-entering service and continuing to serve until 1957. In the background, outside the East Yorkshire School of Motoring (no association with the bus operator of that name), a Ford Anglia carries a huge signboard on the roof as well as the customary L plates displayed on a vehicle used for driving tuition. *Geoff Warnes*

Opposite top Whilst Christ Church is often considered to have been a terminal point for buses from independently owned fleets, the Corporation had a share in services to Armthorpe and Stainforth which departed from there. On 7 August 1956, 89 is waiting to depart to Armthorpe on the service operated jointly with Blue Line and Felix Motors. It is a Daimler CWA6 with Weymann utility bodywork, delivered in August 1943 but, curiously in view of the shortage of new buses during the war, stored and not placed into service until February 1945. *Geoff Warnes*

Opposite The last new bus to utility standard supplied to Doncaster (albeit with upholstered seats from new) was 90, a Bristol K6A with Strachans bodywork, which entered service in March 1946. Due to its lowbridge layout, it was mainly used on the service to Edlington and when the low bridge problem was resolved in 1957, it was withdrawn along with several of the Corporation's other lowbridge double-deckers. The words LOW BRIDGE above the front fleet number can clearly be seen in this picture of it, shortly before withdrawal, in Glasgow Paddocks Bus Station, waiting to depart on its regular service. In the background, an East Midland Leyland Royal Tiger almost obscures a Leyland PD2 of the same operator. The PD2 still carries the distinctive chrome yellow and chocolate livery, replaced by red in 1956. *Geoff Warnes*

In the early post-war period, like many municipal fleets, Doncaster received a batch of Leyland PD2s with bodywork constructed in Leyland's own workshop. 96 was the last of a batch of four, and entered service in March 1948. It was photographed on 10 March 1956 in Trafford Street Bus Station, operating on the service to Highfields. Both it and Bristol K6A 100 behind retain the three cream band livery which was being phased out at the time. In 1963 these four PD2s (plus 2 similar buses delivered in 1951) were considered to have sound enough chassis to receive newer Roe bodies transferred from redundant trolleybuses. *Geoff Warnes*

This is 96 in its later guise after receiving the 1955 Roe body from trolleybus 398. In order to accommodate a 27ft body on what is nominally a 26ft chassis, it was necessary to move the front bulkhead back a few inches and set back the new windscreen a little, producing a distinctive peak effect. Despite this it was still possible to retain the original seating capacity of 62. Number 96 would continue to provide useful service for the Corporation until October 1973. Even then it was not finished, as work was carried out to convert it to a recovery vehicle and tree lopper, though it did not enter service in this form until after the formation of SYPTE. *Mike Russell*

Doncaster's final delivery of Bristols came in the winter of 1947/8 when four Roe bodied K6As (97-100) entered service. Prior to the opening of the Doncaster By-Pass in 1961, the A1 Great North Road passed through the centre of the town and as traffic volumes grew, congestion became a serious issue for the Transport Department. This was particularly so during the St Leger Festival in September when thousands of racegoers added to the problem. In September 1960 when this photograph was taken, one of the solutions was to divert certain services away from their normal town centre termini to a temporary terminus in the Market Place in order to avoid them crossing the A1. This included the trolleybus services to Beckett Road and Wheatley Hills, and as there was no trolleybus wiring at this point, motor buses had to be substituted. The displaced trolleybuses provided extra capacity on the Race Course route. Bristol 98 is loading for a trip to Wheatley Hills. *Geoff Warnes*

On the same day Daimler CVD6 115 is loading in the Market Place at a temporary stand for the service to Beckett Road. As this was normally a trolleybus route, the Daimler evidently did not have "Beckett Road" on its destination blind and has a paper sticker in its front nearside widow instead. To the right of the bus, an Inspector chats to the crew during a lull in activity. In the background, AECs 154 and 157 wait to depart to Intake and Leicester Avenue respectively, whilst to the left a Thornycroft lorry of Mason's storefitters stands outside Timothy Whites chemists shop. Doncaster bought 20 Roe-bodied Daimler CVD6s in 1948/9, of which 18 were highbridge buses like 115, whilst two (111/112) were lowbridge for the service to Edlington. *Geoff Warnes*

Doncaster's deliveries in 1951 were a mixed bag. As well as a pair of 8ft-wide double-deckers (one AEC and one Daimler), the Corporation took delivery of an early underfloor-engined single-decker, 21, an AEC Regal IV with Roe bodywork. As originally built, it featured a central entrance/exit for operation with a conductor, but was rarely used in regular service and was generally confined to schools and works services. In 1960 it was rebuilt with a separate entrance at the front and converted for one man operation. In this form it was photographed alongside the motor bus depot on Grandstand Road. Never very popular, it went for scrap in 1965. *Roger Holmes*

Also in 1951 came two Leyland-bodied PD2/1s (123/124) similar to the batch of four already in service. Out of service with a flat offside front tyre and looking somewhat neglected, 123 was photographed in West Laith Gate shortly before being rebuilt with the 1958 Roe body from trolleybus 353. With its second body it would continue in service until 1970. *Paul Roberts*

Unimpressed by Regal IV 21, Doncaster reverted to front-engined half-cab layout for its 1953 delivery of single-deckers. They were AEC Regal IIIs with 9.6 litre engine and constant mesh gearbox, mechanically very similar to a batch of Regent III double-deckers received at the same time. 22-24 were 30ft-long 39-seaters for the joint service to Sheffield that was restricted to single-deckers due to a very low bridge at Meadowhall. After the Sheffield service was rerouted in 1956 to avoid the low bridge, the Regals were soon converted for one-man operation. 24 is seen in 1959 in Young Street prior to entering Glasgow Paddocks Bus Station for a trip to Edlington, almost certainly duplicating the regular service. *Geoff Warnes*

Of the twelve AEC Regent IIIs delivered in 1953, ten had full height Roe bodies as illustrated by 129, pictured emerging from Sandringham Road on the service from Intake. After issues with the two 8ft-wide double-deckers new in 1951, Doncaster reverted to a 7ft 6in width for these deliveries. Indeed the two 8ft- wide double-deckers were sold to local independent operators in 1955. Like the two 8-footers, these buses had a second step on to the platform, which was at the same level as the lower saloon floor. The passenger seats were of the Sidhil-Morseat patented design in which the window-side passenger sat at a slight angle away from the window, shoulders overlapping those of the gangway-side passenger, thereby minimising overhang into the gangway. *Geoff Warnes*

When the Doncaster – Sheffield route was rerouted to accommodate double-deckers, Doncaster's share tended to be in the hands of the more powerful Regent IIIs, rather than the lightweight Regent Vs, which struggled on the hills. One of the former, 128, is passing a huge dragline of Lehane, Mackenzie and Shand, main contractors for the construction of the A1(M) Doncaster By-pass which is taking shape in the background. *Geoff Warnes*

The other two 1953 AEC Regent IIIs had Roe lowbridge bodies for use on the Edlington service. Of these, 135 is waiting to depart from Glasgow Paddocks Bus Station in May 1959 on its usual route. By this time the offending bridge had been removed and the service could be run by normal height buses. Consequently 135 was sold later that year to Cooper Bros of South Kirkby for use on the United Services operation between Doncaster and Wakefield. Painted in a mid blue livery, it continued to run into Doncaster on a regular basis until 1971. *Geoff Warnes*

In his quest to control operating costs General Manager Tom Bamford standardised on the 7ft 6in-wide lightweight AEC Regent V with 7.7-litre engine and synchromesh gearbox for double deck deliveries between 1955 and 1961, building up a fleet of 31. All had Roe bodywork, with teak framework to the lower deck and alloy-framed upper deck to keep the weight down. With an unladen weight of around 6 tons 15 cwts, these buses performed adequately on Doncaster's flat terrain, carrying up to 62 seated (65 in later deliveries) plus eight standing passengers in somewhat cramped conditions. Number 158 of the second batch delivered in 1957 stands outside the grocery store of Hodgson & Hepworth, whose business interests in Victorian times included the operation of horse buses. To the right, demolition work has taken place in preparation for the construction of the Arndale Centre. *Jim Sambrooks*

One man operation on core services commenced in December 1961 when the trolleybus service to Hyde Park was converted to diesel operation, followed by the service to Hexthorpe in March 1962. To operate these a batch of 6 AEC Reliances (25-30) was obtained. These were fitted with metal-framed Roe bodies to Park Royal design. 26 is seen loading in West Street for the short journey to Hexthorpe. With a narrow entrance, high floor and an unpleasant level of vibration, these buses compared unfavourably with the tracklesses they replaced. After nine years the whole batch was withdrawn and sold, finding homes with independent operators around the country; 26, for example, would spend eight years with Red Rover, Aylesbury. *Mike Russell*

Doncaster's next batch of single-deckers for one-man operation arrived in 1963. This time the Corporation turned to Leyland to supply five Tiger Cubs with 45-seat Roe bodies, numbered 31-35. In 1967, in the hope of attracting additional revenues from private hire work, 31 and 32 exchanged seats for a more comfortable set from the 1953 Regal IIIs. At the same time they had a bizarre cream flash applied to the side panels, reminiscent of the 1930s and 40s fashion for swoops, which ignored the shape of the bodywork. In this condition, 31 is seen leaving the Northern Bus Station with a good load on the service to Highfields in August 1968. These Tiger Cubs were successful vehicles but a subsequent standardisation on dual-door buses for one-man operation restricted their use in later times. *Geoffrey Morant*

By the end of 1959 Doncaster had a standard fleet of 28 Karrier or Sunbeam W trolleybuses all with modern Roe bodywork fitted between 1954 and 1959. When the Transport Committee voted to replace the trolleys with motor buses, the remarkable decision was made to transfer the most recently built bodies on to diesel chassis, and 12 Daimler CVG6 chassis were ordered, having similar dimensions to the trolleybuses. The resulting combination, though noticeably tall and narrow, was a useful and attractive bus. The first, 168, entered service in June 1962, with the Roe body from trolleybus 386. It is seen here in West Laith Gate during the period of gradual replacement of trolleybuses on the Balby service. The similarity with the trolleybus bus behind is clear. In this form 168 had a full life, completing more than 13 years service in Doncaster and serving SYPTE before withdrawal in 1975. *Richard Simons*

Whilst 167, numerically the last of 31 Roe bodied lightweight AEC Regent Vs, drops off on Warmsworth Road in Balby, Daimler 'convert' 172 picks up across the road on its way back to town. The Daimler carries the 1958 Roe body transferred from trolleybus 370 and entered service one month before trolleybuses ceased to run to Balby in September 1962. It is being overtaken by a tanker of United Coke & Chemicals Co Ltd. The Regent, new in 1960 and one of the last exposed radiator AECs to enter service in the UK, would be sold off prematurely in 1970, a victim of the drive towards one-man operation, and would spend the next year or so running for Andy's Coaches of Birmingham. *Geoff Warnes*

In 1962, looking to increase capacity on certain services, Doncaster ordered eight 30ft-long forward-entrance double-deckers. The chassis order was split equally between Leyland and Daimler. The Leylands, with 9.8 litre O.600 engines, were capable of a good performance on the hilly joint service to Sheffield and were often to be found on it. 174 is seen returning from Sheffield, descending Barrow Road on the diversion that was adopted to avoid the very low bridge at Meadowhall. There was just enough clearance under this bridge (and a second one just out of sight round the corner) for most double-deckers but the Doncaster trolleybus 'converts' were too tall and could not be allocated to the route. *Graham Hague*

Like the Leylands, the four Daimler CVG6/30s ordered in 1962 had forward-entrance bodywork by Roe, which had become the Corporation's regular coachbuilder. One of these, 178, is setting off from the Northern Bus Station in July 1971 on the short run to Castle Hills Road. This service, requiring one bus (two on Saturdays) was shared with Yorkshire Traction and periodically the provision of the bus would switch between operators. The steel girders on the car park above the bus station had been given a special coating so that they would never need to be repainted, but this had the effect of making them look rusty and neglected. *Geoffrey Morant*

In 1963, Leyland was prevailed upon to provide two new PD2/40 Special chassis, built to a width of 7ft 6in to accommodate bodywork transferred from further trolleybuses. These were delivered as numbers 188 and 189, of which the latter is seen approaching the town centre along Thorne Road in June 1970. The Roe bodywork was previously fitted to Sunbeam trolleybus 394, the chassis of which had been acquired from the Mexborough & Swinton Traction Company. *Omnibus Society/Peter Henson*

The 30ft-long Daimlers, fitted with Gardner 6LW engines and preselector gearboxes, were more suited to the flatter terrain to the north and east of Doncaster. In this May 1973 picture 180, in the later, brighter livery, is turning into Printing Office Street, approaching the town centre terminus of the service to Beckett Road. These buses, together with the Leyland PD3s, entered service with 72 seats with a maximum of five standing allowed in line with prevailing agreements. However it was soon appreciated that, as the agreement allowed up to eight standees on buses with 70 seats, the overall capacity could be increased by one if a pair of seats was removed. In line with the Department's reputation for parsimony, this took place in 1964. *Omnibus Society/Roy Marshall*

Looking to extend the level of one-man operation, Doncaster sought a vehicle of intermediate length, fitted with two doors to minimise dwell times at busy stops, but capable of carrying up to 60 passengers. To meet this specification, Leyland supplied the Royal Tiger Cub, a model intended primarily for export markets. A batch of ten, fitted with Roe bodywork seating 45 and with a standing capacity of 15, entered service in 1965. Though badged as Tiger Cubs, the Royal Tiger Cubs had O.600 engines and slotted between the short and long versions of the Leopard in terms of length. 39 is waiting to depart on the service to Skellow (Owston Park). Despite the destination, the Owston Park terminus was in Carcroft and the bus would not reach the village of Skellow. The picture date is May 1970. *Omnibus Society/Roy Marshall*

A second batch of Royal Tiger Cubs arrived in 1968. These differed from the first delivery in having a more modern style of bodywork and pneumocyclic gearboxes, compared to the synchromesh units in the earlier buses. These buses were particularly associated with the Bentley service, and 52 is seen in June 1971 leaving the Northern Bus Station with a typical standing load. A Leyland Leopard of WR & P Bingley is following on United Services' service to Wakefield. A particularly large road sign dominates the background. *Geoffrey Morant*

When Robert Davies was appointed to replace the retiring Tom Bamford as General Manager in 1969, he set about modernising the Department's image. He commissioned the local College of Art to produce a design for updating the livery whilst retaining the basic colour. The result was considered quite startling at the time – consisting of the addition of a broad purple stripe outlined in white. It first appeared on Daimler Fleetline 208 and, receiving general approval, was gradually applied to the rest of the fleet. Fleetlines 208 and 209 were never equipped for one-man operation. Fitted with 78-seat bodies by Roe, they entered service in 1967, often appearing on the routes to Sheffield and Rossington, which remained crew-operated for many years. *Geoffrey Morant*

The first dual-door double deckers arrived in 1969 for the conversion of the Edlington route to one-man operation. Six Daimler Fleetlines, with rather plain bodywork by Roe were numbered 210-215. On the occasion illustrated above, in May 1971, 210 is carrying racegoers back to the town centre at the end of a busy day at the racecourse. The sticker in the foremost nearside window indicates a special fare of 4p – this would be 2p more than that charged on the regular Hyde Park or Racecourse circulars. *Omnibus Society/Roy Marshall*

223 carries the highest fleet number allocated to a Doncaster motor bus. The last of a batch of eight Daimler Fleetlines with Roe bodies (built to a Park Royal design) obtained in 1970, it is waiting to depart on the service to Broomhouse Lane in June of that year. These particular buses were too tall to pass under the railway bridges on Barrow Road on the Sheffield route, and were unable to run to Edlington until an offending bridge was removed. *Omnibus Society/Peter Henson*

The launch of the Seddon Pennine RU offered a lower wider entrance and a 60-passenger capacity (42 seated; 18 standing) within a 33ft overall length. With the promise of quick delivery and a competitive price, Doncaster ordered 14 with lightweight Seddon bodywork. Put to work on some of Doncaster's busiest services, they soon revealed shortcomings in the design, centred on the brakes and transmission. An appropriate maintenance regime was put in place, though the bodywork was starting to show signs of structural weakness by the time the fleet passed into the hands of South Yorkshire Passenger Transport Executive on 1 April 1974. 61 is seen pulling on to the A630 from the Winning Post terminus of the Balby service on 17 June 1972. It has had the cream areas of paintwork overpainted red in preparation for the application of the purple stripe. *Geoff Warnes*

Doncaster placed a further order for Seddon Pennine RU chassis. These were fitted with more substantial bodywork by Roe, and proved to be the only buses of Seddon manufacture to be bodied at Crossgates. In May 1973 No. 77 is seen passing along Waterdale on its way to undertake a journey on the infrequent variation of the Balby service to St Peters Road, as indicated by the destination board wedged at a jaunty angle in the nearside windscreen. On the extreme right, a sign indicates that car parking is available for the sum of 10p per day on the site of the former Glasgow Paddocks bus station. *Omnibus Society/Roy Marshall*

In 1973, Doncaster acquired further Seddons – but these were front-engined Pennine IV 236 Midi buses, again with 25-seat bodywork by Seddon. Three were received in May and were used to inaugurate a service to the rapidly expanding housing estate at West Bessacarr, where the road network was deemed unsuitable for full size buses. Whilst the timetable required only a single bus, a second was kept on standby in the bus station in case the demand exceeded the capacity of the service bus. Brand new 23 is leaving the Southern Bus Station on the service for which it was obtained. It is passing a late model Bristol MW of Lincolnshire Road Car, which is on layover before returning to Scunthorpe. Two more Seddon midi buses arrived in November 1973 to operate a new Inner Circle service and were the last acquisitions of Doncaster's Transport Department. *Omnibus Society/Peter Henson*

Rotherham

The Borough of Rotherham gained powers to operate tramcars in 1900 and services commenced in January 1903. The network grew rapidly and in addition to serving the borough included joint services both with Sheffield Corporation (to Sheffield) and the Mexborough & Swinton Tramways Co (to Parkgate).

The tramway network reached its maximum extent in 1912, the same year that the first trolleybus service commenced, feeding the Broom tram terminus from the growing villages of Maltby, Bramley and Wickersley, which were outside the borough boundary. In the following year, the first motor bus service was started, running from the town centre to the outlying village of Thorpe Hesley. Additional services followed, but further growth was stifled by the outbreak of the First World War. Although the first four motor buses, of Daimler manufacture, were built as double-deckers, the Corporation thenceforth standardised on single-deckers for all subsequent deliveries until after the end of World War 2.

The Corporation also sought opportunities further afield and in December 1926 commenced a through service to Barnsley, via Hoyland, jointly with the Barnsley & District Traction Co. In July 1927 a service from Doncaster through Rotherham to Sheffield was introduced, with operation shared by the three municipalities. By 1929, the Maltby route was still the only trolleybus service but a decision was then made to replace the tram network with trolleybuses. The Mexborough & Swinton company was also looking to do the same and, under a revised agreement, Corporation trolleybuses took a share in through running to Mexborough and Conisbrough. Meanwhile the motor bus fleet was becoming standardised on vehicles of Bristol manufacture, also with single-deck centre entrance bodywork.

During the 1930s, most of the remaining tramway services were converted to trolleybus operation, the exception being the joint route to Sheffield (together with the short working to Templeborough). As Sheffield was firmly wedded to tramcars, Rotherham bought 11 unusual single-ended tramcars to operate its share of the service and they ran until the final closure of tramcar operation in the town in 1949. The Transport Department had no buses built to the Ministry of Supply's so-called utility specification, the last vehicles of pre-war standard entering service in February 1943. At the end of hostilities the fleet consisted entirely of Bristol single-deckers – 42 L5Gs and 24 JO5Gs, plus a few earlier J types, all with 32 seat centre-entrance bodywork.

New General Manager Norman Rylance ordered double-deckers for the first time in more than 30 years. Four Bristol K types were received in December 1946 and more came each year until the type became unavailable. In 1949 additional double-deckers were urgently required to replace the trams on the jointly operated route to Sheffield and 12 Crossley double-deckers, built for Liverpool, were obtained. Rotherham then bought more Crossleys, Bristol chassis no longer being available to the open market. The trolleybus fleet was also in need of modernisation but at this stage the adoption of double-deckers was impractical because of low bridges on the network. A total of 44 new Daimler six-wheel single deck trolleybuses entered service in 1949 and 1950, replacing all but two of the pre-war fleet.

When, in 1954, it was announced that the trolleybus service to Maltby would be cut back to terminate at Wickersley, with motor buses taking over the section beyond, it appeared that the future for electric traction was bleak. However, in 1955 the decision was made to rebuild 20 of the Daimler single-deck trolleys with new Roe double-deck bodies. A handful of single-deckers remained for the joint routes to Mexborough and Conisbrough until motor buses took over in 1961. The double-deckers were successful and trolleybuses continued to run in Rotherham until 1965.

Meanwhile, the motor bus network was expanding to serve new housing developments in and around the borough. The Daimler CVG6, with Gardner engine and Wilson preselector gearbox became the double-decker of choice. From 1959 the forward-entrance 70 seat version was adopted and by the end of 1966 no fewer than 52 of these were in service. The AEC Reliance chassis was chosen for single-deck orders, for use on services that were impassable to double-deckers.

In 1967 the Department bowed to the inevitable and placed its first rear-engined buses in service. Predictably the model chosen was the Daimler Fleetline with bodywork constructed by Charles H. Roe of Leeds. This combination formed the basis all further double-deck deliveries before the undertaking was absorbed by the South Yorkshire PTE on 1 April 1974.

Rotherham built up a large fleet of Bristol single-deckers in the late 1930s, and rebuilt many of them after the war to extend their useful lives. 143 was one such, and is seen preparing to leave Doncaster's Glasgow Paddocks Bus Station on 2 March 1956 with a full load. This 37-seat bus, a 1938 L5G, was unique in that the rebuild had involved removing the original body, extending the chassis and fitting new bodywork constructed in Rotherham's own workshops, using framework supplied by East Lancashire Coach Builders. The Doncaster – Rotherham – Sheffield service would be converted to double-deck operation on 1 July 1956, by-passing the low railway bridge on Meadowhall Road. *Geoff Warnes*

The Transport Department retained several of its fleet of pre-war Bristols for ancillary duties long after their passenger-carrying duties had come to an end. One such survivor was BET 515, an L5G with Cravens bodywork, new in 1938. Upon withdrawal from service in 1955 it was retained as a driver instruction vehicle, and continued to perform this function until 1967. It is seen in the yard of Rawmarsh Road depot carrying an oversize L plate on its dull grey livery. *Michael Fowler*

The last new trolleybuses to enter service in Rotherham were six-wheel single deckers of Daimler manufacture, 44 of which arrived during 1949-50. These had centre-entrance bodywork by East Lancashire, many being assembled at the East Lancs factory in Bridlington. This large delivery allowed for the replacement of almost all pre-war trolleybus stock. At this time the trolleybus fleet consisted entirely of single-deck vehicles due to the presence of several low bridges on the network. It was believed that this design, featuring a central entrance/exit position, minimised dwell times at stops and allowed for faster running. In the photograph above, trolleybus 84 is standing at the Park Lane, Thrybergh terminus of cross-town service 6 from Kimberworth. It would be renumbered 2 in 1957, and after withdrawal in 1960 was exported to Spain and ran for use in San Sebastian until 1971. *Geoff Warnes*

During 1956/7 Rotherham had 20 of its postwar Daimler single-deck trolleybuses rebodied by Roe as double-deckers, leaving just enough single-deckers in service to cover the routes to Mexborough and Conisbrough which were operated jointly with the Mexborough & Swinton company. One of the trolleys which remained in service in its original form was FET 609, renumbered in 1957 from 9 to 5. It is seen on Saturday 25 March 1961 passing the South Yorkshire Hotel along Swinton Road, before construction of the Mexborough by-pass caused this section of road to become a cul-de-sac. Motor buses would take over operation of these services on the following Monday. *Geoff Warnes*

From 1924 trolleybuses ran the seven miles from Rotherham town centre to Maltby, until 1954, when the section beyond Wickersley was abandoned in favour of motor buses. The trackless service was maintained as far as Wickersley and number 25 is waiting at the Wickersley terminus prior to returning to town on 11 July 1962. It is one of the 20 Daimler CTE6 single-deckers of 1949-50 that were rebuilt and rebodied as double-deckers by Roe in 1956-7, in which form it survived until the end of the system in 1965. *Paul Creswell*

Daimler trolleybus 33 glides along Masbrough Street, heading towards the town centre from Kimberworth. Station Road, running off to the right behind the trolleybus leads to Masbrough station which was Rotherham's principal railway station at the time, but since closed. Of note is the bright pink Thames delivery truck, a reminder of days when many people heated their homes with paraffin. The trolleybus is running on the cross-town service to Thrybergh. Curiously, cross-town fares were not available, through passengers having to pay again from the town centre. This practice continued after conversion to motor bus operation right up to the commencement of one-man operation in 1986.
Robin Helliar-Symons

Bristol 180 is standing at the Chapeltown Park Gates terminus of service 16 from Rotherham. Originally built in 1949 as an L6B with Bruce single-deck bodywork, in 1951 it was rebuilt as a double-decker with a new body by East Lancashire Coach Builders, whilst the two-year-old Bruce single-deck body was used to modernise one of the pre-war L5Gs. Service 16 was an extension of the first motor bus route operated by the Corporation to Thorpe Hesley in July 1913. In this view, 180 had been duplicated by one of the Weymann-bodied lowbridge Daimlers (124-128) delivered in 1955. Rotherham was an early advocate of the sliding cab door – particularly uncommon on Bristol chassis. *Ian Wild*

Rotherham also sourced new double-deckers from Crossley. The first batch of twelve, on DD42/7 chassis were hurriedly obtained in 1949. These were part of an order for Liverpool which had delayed delivery on half the order and Crossley sold the completed buses, building new ones for Liverpool at a later date. Rotherham bought them when additional buses were suddenly required when it was decided not to reinstate the tram service to Sheffield. One of this first batch, 196, is standing next to 211, an 8ft-wide DD42/8 of the last batch delivered in 1953. Like all the undertaking's Crossleys, they were fitted with Crossley bodywork. *Geoffrey Morant*

Standing in All Saints' Square prior to departing on a journey on service 25 along Moorgate Road to Whiston is Bristol K6B 199. Rotherham continued to favour Gardner 5LW engines for its single-deck Bristols, but unusually for a municipal operator, adopted the six-cylinder Bristol AVW engine for double-deck deliveries. 199 was one of six K6Bs built in 1949 with bodywork constructed in Bridlington by the Yorkshire Equipment Company using frames supplied by East Lancashire Coach Builders. This organisation, which had constructed air-sea rescue boats and other small craft for the RAF and Royal Navy, would soon be taken over by East Lancs and renamed East Lancashire Coach Builders (Bridlington) Ltd. *Ken Jubb*

Having placed orders several years in advance for the supply of bus chassis, Rotherham was the only operator outside the Tilling group to receive examples of the Bristol KS6B. Twelve entered service in 1950/51 with bodywork constructed by East Lancs (Bridlington). In this view from May 1967, 105 is leaving from All Saints' Square with a full load on service 22 to Braithwell. *Ken Jubb*

On 19 February 1966, its side panels covered with road dirt, 110 was photographed passing the Rotherham Co-operative Society grocery store on Canklow Road, operating on service 30 to the Three Magpies Hotel at Brinsworth. It is another of the Bristol KS6Bs with East Lancs (Bridlington) bodywork. It is Saturday afternoon and the Co-op is closed, as evidenced by the wooden gate fixed across the entrance. Number 110 would be withdrawn in the following year and sold for scrap. *Geoff Warnes*

Early post-war deliveries of single-deckers were a mixture of Bristol L5G and L6B chassis, with centre-entrance half-canopy bodywork constructed by Bruce or East Lancs (Bridlington) to similar design. The L6Bs were all rebuilt as double-deckers within a few years but the L5Gs (with less powerful five-cylinder engines) were retained in their original form in order to maintain those services for which single-deckers were still required. L5G 119 of 1950 was photographed in Barnsley Bus Station in July 1961, illustrating the outdated appearance of these buses. Several Yorkshire Traction buses appear in the background, whilst on the extreme left, a Roe-bodied Leyland PD2/3 of the Yorkshire Woollen District Transport Co is visible in its all red livery. *Geoff Warnes*

Rotherham 112 passes the Rootes Group car dealership on Corporation Street, where a new Hillman Imp, amongst other models, is for sale in the showroom. It is another Bristol L6B, built as a single-decker in 1950, but rebodied as a double-decker in 1952 after less than two years service in its original form. It is on Service 18 from Blackburn, a community lying between Rotherham and Sheffield, sadly dissected by the construction of the M1 motorway. *Ken Jubb*

Following the nationalisation of the Tilling Group, Bristol bus chassis were no longer available on the open market. Rotherham received its outstanding orders and then turned to Crossley for further deliveries of double-deckers, evidently having had a satisfactory operating experience with the twelve buses diverted from Liverpool. A further six DD42/7s of similar design to the earlier twelve entered service in May 1951. One of these, number 204, is pulling out of Bridgegate on service 18 to Blackburn during 1965. Though still in excellent condition, it would be withdrawn at the beginning of the following year and sold for scrap. *Michael Fowler*

Six more Crossleys entered service during 1953. These were DD42/8 models – the first 8ft-wide buses for Rotherham but the last Crossley chassis to enter service in the UK. One of them, 210, is seen in April 1968 outside the Angel Hotel in Bridgegate, waiting to depart on service 70 to Templeborough. This was essentially a short working of the joint service 69 to Sheffield, catering primarily for workers at the steel plants within the Rotherham boundary. *Omnibus Society/Roy Marshall*

No longer able to buy Bristol or Crossley motor bus chassis, Rotherham turned to Daimler, the supplier of its post-war trolleybus fleet. In 1954 a fleet of 15 CVG6s was received, fitted with Gardner 6LW engines, Wilson preselector gearboxes and handsome Weymann five-bay bodywork. In this view, 219 stands on the gentle slope of Corporation Street outside the All Saints Building. A chock (fastened to the cab by a cord) has been placed under the front wheel to prevent it from rolling down the hill while it is unattended by the crew. The All Saints Building was demolished in 2008 and replaced by an open space known as Minster Gardens. *Ken Jubb*

The move away from single-deck operation took another step forward in September 1955 when services to Brinsworth and Treeton were converted to double-deck, using a second batch of new Daimler CVG6s, 124-128. These had lowbridge bodywork by Weymann, and were the first low height double-deckers in the fleet. Despite their inconvenient internal layout, these buses survived until 1971, by which time they had received the later livery style, with blue bonnets and cream applied to the upper deck panels and the addition of a "Rotherham Corporation" fleetname above the coat of arms. 126 displays this later livery in the yard at Rawmarsh Road depot in August 1970. *Omnibus Society/Roy Marshall*

Rotherham took delivery of a further ten Daimler CVG6s in 1957. Three of these had lowbridge bodywork by Roe, whilst the other seven had full height bodies built by Weymann. In this March 1967 picture, one of the latter (234) is seen leaving Doncaster Southern Bus Station on service 77 to Sheffield, a route with which these buses were associated for many years. On the left, Doncaster AEC Reliance 27 is picking up for a journey to Edlington, evidently a duplicate to the normal service as a board in the windscreen indicates it is going to Edlington Shops Only. There seems to have been little concern about the safety risks of constructing the multi-storey car park above an active bus station. *Geoffrey Morant*

Rotherham 164 was an AEC Reliance delivered in 1957. This example, along with 165, had bodywork constructed by Park Royal Vehicles but with interiors fitted out by Roe. It is leaving the temporary open bus station (which occupied part of the site of the current Interchange and multi-storey car park) on former trolleybus service 54 to Greasbrough, which passed under a low railway bridge at the bottom of Car Hill precluding the use of double-deckers. This May 1969 view illustrates a version of the livery which featured a larger expanse of cream, carried by some of the Reliances for a while. *Omnibus Society/ Roy Marshall*

Whilst the Corporation favoured Daimlers for its double-deck fleet, it had a need for some buses of slightly lower overall height that could pass under some of the railway bridges on its network. As Daimler did not offer a suitable product, it turned to AEC to supply its low height integrally-constructed Bridgemaster, five of which were received early in 1961. Fleet number 139 is leaving All Saints Square on service 19 to Dinnington in May 1968. Alternate journeys on this service, which was shared with East Midland, ran through to Worksop, passing under the low bridge at Anston. Arguably, the application of Rotherham's livery helped to disguise the box-like appearance of the body. *Omnibus Society/Roy Marshall*

In need of further low height double-deckers, the Corporation turned again to AEC, which supplied three examples of the Renown in 1964. With bodywork constructed by Roe to Park Royal design, 90 makes its way to the stand to load for a trip to the post-war housing estate at East Herringthorpe. A setting-down restriction along Doncaster Road would lead to a speedy outward journey. By this time the need for low-height buses had diminished due to highway alterations and bridge removal, and these buses were being utilised more widely across the network. *Ken Jubb*

Between 1959 and 1966, the Department's preferred choice for double-deckers of conventional height was the Daimler CVG6/30 with Gardner 6LX engine and forward entrance bodywork, seating 70 passengers. 146 was one of three built with Metro-Cammell all-metal bodywork to the Orion design. It is waiting on the Maltby stand on Effingham Street. The stop, with its basic tubular barriers, had been sited in the era of rear-entrance buses, and as a result the back of 146 is very close to a zebra crossing and the junction of Howard Street. In the background, construction is taking place on a new store for C&A, as well as a new market building. The picture was taken in August 1970. *Omnibus Society/Roy Marshall*

The temporary bus station off Frederick Street has slightly more of an air of permanence here, although it would soon be disrupted again for the construction of a multi-storey car park above. Bus 156 was one of the final trio of AEC Reliances delivered to the Corporation – these had Willowbrook bodies to a BET design that was somewhat outdated by the time they entered service in 1964. Replaced by new Seddons in 1972, all three of these Reliances passed to Primrose Valley of Filey for further service, conveying holidaymakers to and from the nearby caravan sites and camps. *Omnibus Society/Roy Marshall*

Bus 71 emerges from under Canklow railway bridge on its way to Brinsworth on Service 31. The bridge actually consists of two structures side by side, the stone arch on the far side having been supplemented by the steel structure on this side. Double-deck buses have to pass under the arch in the centre of the road. 71 is a Daimler CVG6LX/30 with Roe bodywork, one of twenty received in 1965 to complete the conversion of trolleybus services to diesel traction. It wears a later version of the livery with cream applied on the between-deck panels and a blue bonnet. *Barry Ridge*

In the original livery application for the type, 61 crosses into Fitzalan Square in Sheffield city centre in April 1969. With the destination blinds set for a journey on service 87 from Sheffield to Maltby, it appears to be running light to the Central Bus Station to take up service. The Daimler CVG6LX/30 with Roe composite bodywork is one of nine similar buses that entered service in December 1966: subsequent orders for Daimlers were for the rear-engined Fleetline model. *Omnibus Society/Roy Marshall*

In 1966 the Corporation also took delivery of three AEC Regent Vs with bodywork constructed in Sheffield by Neepsend Coachworks to East Lancs design – Neepsend Coachworks was set up by the John Brown group, which had acquired the Cravens business and at the time also owned East Lancashire Coach Builders of Blackburn. With 11.3-litre engines and semi-automatic gearboxes they were fast and powerful buses, well-suited to the interurban service between Sheffield and Doncaster on which number 130 is seen in August 1970. Being non-standard, they had short lives in Rotherham and were withdrawn in 1973, though they survived to pass into SYPTE ownership. Sold off without further use, two of them (including 130) passed to Morris Brothers of Swansea, whilst the third joined them after a spell with A1 Service in Scotland. *Omnibus Society/ Peter Henson*

From 1967, the Corporation adopted the Roe bodied Daimler Fleetline as its standard bus and all future double-deck deliveries were of this combination. After two batches of single-door examples came ten dual-door models, intended for one-man operation of intensive town services. Numerically the first of these, 199, is crossing Chantry Bridge over the River Don in May 1970, having just left the bus station on its way to Blackburn. On the left, the presence of scaffolding indicates that restoration work is being carried out on the Chapel of Our Lady on the Bridge. *Omnibus Society/Peter Henson*

Bus 170 is leaving the bus station on service 48 to Barrow Colliery at Worsbrough, near Barnsley. It is a single-deck version of the Daimler Fleetline, one of a pair with Willowbrook coachwork delivered in 1970 and fitted with semi-coach seating. In the background, double-deck Fleetline 200 is loading passengers for a short but busy trip to the pre-war estate at East Dene. Situated beneath a concrete multi-storey car park, Rotherham bus station was always a gloomy place, especially on a wet day such as this, sometime in 1973. *Geoffrey Morant*

Daimler Fleetline 217 turns from Howard Street past the then town hall into Frederick Street, in an area of the town centre that would subsequently be pedestrianised. With dual-door bodywork to the more modern design adopted by Roe (and Park Royal) from around 1970, twenty seven buses of this type entered service during 1971/2, accelerating the switch to one-man operation. The side destination blind is set to read Pay As You Enter Exact Fare Please in this June 1971 picture. *Omnibus Society/Peter Henson*

An unexpected choice to replace the remaining AEC Reliances was the Seddon Pennine RU. Nine buses of this type arrived in 1972, fitted with Plaxton Derwent coachwork, an unusual choice for a municipal undertaking. In November 1972 173 was picking up in Barnsley Bus Station for the return journey to its home town on service 27, operation of which was shared with Yorkshire Traction. With five-speed gearboxes and high-backed seats, these buses were well-suited for the Corporation's longer distance services. All nine passed to SYPTE in 1974, but by the end of 1981 all had been eliminated, with 173 having been the last active example. *Omnibus Society/Peter Henson*

Yorkshire Traction

Unlike the other major South Yorkshire centres of population, Barnsley never had its own municipal transport and its public transport needs were met almost entirely by private enterprise. A small tramway was opened in 1902, running from Smithies in the north through the town centre to Worsbrough in the south, but in 1930 it was replaced by buses. The tramway was operated by a local subsidiary of the British Electric Traction Company, the Barnsley & District Electric Traction Company Ltd, which dropped the word Electric in 1919 and then became the Yorkshire Traction Company Ltd in 1928.

The later change reflected the expansion which had taken place since the first motorbuses had been introduced in 1913 but mainly during the 1920s, giving the company a presence in all the other urban centres in what was to become South Yorkshire as well as in Huddersfield, Pontefract and Wakefield. Even so, the title overplayed Yorkshire Traction's significance as the company never came close to covering the whole of Yorkshire.

The 1930s were a decade of consolidation when *Tracky*, as it was invariably known locally, took over many smaller concerns. Already it had a near monopoly in Barnsley, running the local town services in much the same way as the corporations did elsewhere. Further afield an extensive network was developed throughout the Dearne Valley area, where the company soon saw off the Dearne District Light Railways, a curious interurban tramway instigated by the urban district councils of Bolton-upon-Dearne, Thurnscoe, Wath-upon-Dearne and Wombwell, which began operation in 1924 but came to an ignominious end nine years later.

In the late 1930s the company built a spacious bus station in Barnsley town centre and all operators were welcomed into it. Every bus service in Barnsley used it and as late as the 1960s buses of more than a dozen operators could be seen there. This was ideal for passengers but a downside for historians is that it proved such a magnet for bus photographers that the town centre streets were largely overlooked. It was a bustling and characterful place, surrounded by railway lines, one of them elevated, and with two adjacent railway stations. Only in the 1970s did it lose most of its atmosphere – the line through Court House Station had long since closed, the number of operators had diminished and the layout was substantially altered.

Not only was Yorkshire Traction the area's largest company operator, it was also one of the most profitable in the BET group (although Mexborough & Swinton did even better). The head office, main depot and central works occupied a large site on Upper Sheffield Road, which originally served as the base for the trams, and the company became one of the town's largest employers. Other depots in South Yorkshire were in Doncaster (opened 1920), Wombwell (1933, formerly the car barns of the Dearne District Light Railways) and Shafton (1934, acquired with Lancashire & Yorkshire Motors), while a handful of buses were based for many years at premises in Royston acquired with the business of Thomas Wombwell in 1933.

With a fleet of more than 300 buses (there were also coaches, for excursions and the important express services), Yorkshire Traction was the second largest operator in South Yorkshire and further expansion came in 1969 (under the National Bus Company) when County Motors and Mexborough & Swinton were taken over. The latter gave the company a much greater presence in Rotherham and the red and cream buses now virtually monopolised the triangle formed by Barnsley, Doncaster and Rotherham.

Leylands dominated the fleet – apart from the inevitable wartime Guy Arabs, some Dennis Lancets in 1949/50 and a pair of Beadle-Commers in the mid 1950s, all new buses from 1935 until 1967 came from the Lancashire manufacturer. Throughout the 1930s and 1940s the fleet was mainly single-deck, a consequence of the many low bridges, but from about 1950 double-deckers were bought in much greater numbers and were used across much of the network. The single/double-deck balance was further altered between 1955 and 1963 by over fifty double-deck conversions from early post-war Leyland PS1 single-deckers. Even so, single-deckers, mainly Leyland Tiger Cubs and later Leopards, remained an important element of the new vehicle intake; the Penistone and Stocksbridge services for example were always out of bounds to double-deckers.

The imposition of National Bus Company corporate livery styles (in this case the poppy red version) in 1973, together with a switch to Bristol VRs and Leyland Nationals, brought *Tracky*'s individuality to an end and the buses featured here are a reminder of an earlier era.

The first double-deckers were Leyland Titan TD1s bought to replace the trams in 1930, and 39 had been acquired by 1942, all but one of them Leyland Titans. Number 722 might look like a Titan but was actually a 1940 Tiger TS8 originally numbered 688. During the wartime blackout its Eastern Coachworks single-deck body was wrecked in an accident and it re-emerged, numbered 722, with the Short Bros double-deck body from a 1932 Daimler CP6. A new Roe lowbridge body was fitted in 1949 and in this form 722 ran until 1959. On 15 May 1959 it was photographed at Glasgow Paddocks, Doncaster, with the blind set for Burghwallis, a small village just off the Great North Road served by infrequent extensions of service 50. *Roger Holmes*

There were few takers in South Yorkshire for Leyland's first post-war double-deck offering, the PD1, and Yorkshire Traction had the largest local fleet – five with Roe bodies in 1946. The only others for South Yorkshire operators were with Doncaster-area independents. The five PD1s lasted until 1961 and in this picture 725 is awaiting its crew outside the offices and canteen in Barnsley Bus Station, the blind indicating a works journey that would not appear in the public timetable. The H after the fleet number indicated a highbridge bus; lowbridge double-deckers had an L suffix. *Geoff Warnes*

Twenty Guy Arabs were delivered between 1943 and 1945, with bodywork from Massey, Northern Counties, Park Royal, Roe and Weymann. The first six were rebodied with lowbridge bodies by Roe in 1950, the next six were similarly treated in 1952 but to highbridge layout and the remainder retained their original bodies. This photograph shows one of the 1952 rebuilds, 713, parked in the middle of Barnsley Bus Station. Coming past it and looking uncannily like a *Tracky* bus, is KHE 526 of Wray (Ideal) of Hoyle Mill. Originally a PS1 coach, it was rebodied by Roe in 1956, getting a new registration number – as did many of *Tracky*'s own PS1s. Behind it is 1010, a 1954 Saunders-Roe bodied Leyland Tiger Cub. *Geoff Warnes*

Deliveries of 32-seat single-deckers resumed in the spring of 1947 and within three years there were 104 Leyland PS1s plus a single PS2. 45 came in 1947, with bodywork from Weymann and Roe, and another 60 in 1949/50, all Brush-bodied except for one from Northern Coachbuilders. Even allowing for the large number of low bridges on the network, this massive investment soon started to look misguided as single-deck bus design advanced rapidly into underfloor-engined models with at least ten more seats. As early as 1955 many of the PS1s were rebuilt and rebodied as double-deckers, while sales of those that remained as single-deck began in 1958. In this March 1956 view Brush-bodied 795 appears to be undertaking an unseasonal excursion to Bridlington. It survived until 1960, a single-decker to the end. *Geoff Warnes*

Opposite The Leyland PD2 was introduced to the fleet in 1948 when five with Leyland bodywork arrived, at a time when the vast majority of the company's new buses were still 32-seat single-deckers. 777 provides an interesting contrast with Sheffield Joint Omnibus Committee's 1143, also a Leyland-bodied PD2 but dating from 1949 and featuring the later body style that had flush-mounted windows. Both buses would head out along Upper Sheffield Road, 777 only as far as Worsbrough Bridge, one of the termini for the long-gone trams, while the SJOC bus would continue to Sheffield. The photograph was taken on 6 June 1963; both buses were withdrawn later in the year. *Roger Holmes*

Yorkshire Traction was one of Leyland Motors' most loyal customers but in 1933/34 bought 23 Dennis Lancets. They proved satisfactory, some lasting into the 1950s, and the company added 30 Lancet IIIs in 1949/50. Six had Windover coach bodies but the balance, delivered in 1950, had Brush bodies to the familiar BET Federation style – the combination was unique to Yorkshire Traction. Four, including numbers 849, 867 and 870, are seen here at the Upper Sheffield Road depot and headquarters on 23 July 1960 when the whole batch was still in stock, the blind displays showing that they performed a wide range of duties. *Geoff Warnes*

The 1950 Leyland PS1s with Brush bodywork were the last of a long line stretching back to the first deliveries of Leyland TS7s in 1935; in the 15-year period nearly 300 broadly similar vehicles entered the fleet. Here at Waterdale, Doncaster, across the road from the departure stands at Glasgow Paddocks, 889 and 895 represent this final batch of half-cab single-deckers. Between them is one of the first batch of Tiger Cubs, Saunders-Roe bodied 1007, new in 1954. The last front-engined single-deckers left the fleet in 1962. *Geoff Warnes*

Fleet additions in 1951 included 929-942, Leyland PD2/1s with Leyland lowbridge bodywork. 934 is seen at Glasgow Paddocks, Doncaster, on 2 March 1956, about to embark on a journey on the lengthy service 22 via Mexborough, Swinton, Wath and Wombwell to Barnsley, which it would reach some 75 minutes later. The basic corrugated shelters at Glasgow Paddocks offered protection from the elements but little else. The East Yorkshire School of Motoring's premises behind the Rover car displayed a logo much the same as the fleetname used by East Yorkshire Motor Services but there was no connection. *Geoff Warnes*

In 1952 Yorkshire Traction took over Cawthorne of Barugh Green's Barnsley to Woolley Colliery service together with two double-deckers. An ex-Doncaster Leyland Titanic lasted only a few months with YTC but the Foden stayed in the fleet until 1959, numbered 128. It had started life as a Foden prototype/demonstrator and been the subject of some changes before it was bought by Cawthorne in 1950. The Willowbrook body dated from 1945 and had originally been on an earlier prototype Foden chassis, while the engine was not the more usual Gardner 6LW but Foden's supercharged two-stroke diesel, notable for its sound. This picture shows it in June 1958 at Waterdale, Doncaster. *Roger Holmes*

By 1953 there were 75 Leyland PD2s in the fleet. Most had bodywork by Leyland or Roe but there were ten 1953 PD2/12s (977-986) with lowbridge bodywork by Northern Counties: the first bodies from this firm apart from four wartime Guy Arabs supplied in 1944/45. Number 982 survived to be renumbered 698 in the 1967 scheme and was withdrawn in 1969. This May 1963 view shows it in Doncaster at the North Bridge terminus of service 94 to Ackworth Moor Top via Skellow and Upton. On departure the bus would perform a U-turn to head north. *Malcolm King*

The first underfloor-engined buses were Leyland Royal Tigers – twenty with Brush bodywork in 1951 (903-922), six with Roe bodies in 1952 (959-964) and ten (992-1001) with Willowbrook bodies in 1953 which took fleet numbers into four digits for the first time. Number 998, seen here on the forecourt of Shafton depot in June 1964, was one of the 1953 batch. It was sold in 1966 although some of the type survived to 1969. To the left is one of the final batch of Leyland Tiger Cubs – six Alexander-bodied examples new in 1962. *Ken Jubb*

The Royal Tiger was rugged but heavy which led to high fuel consumption – often the same as contemporary double-deckers. Its replacement was the lighter and highly successful Tiger Cub and it was *Tracky's* choice from 1954 onwards, starting with 24 with Saunders-Roe bodies (1002-1025). 1023 is seen on layover in Barnsley Bus Station, its blinds indicating a service for miners at Cortonwood Colliery. The match between fleet and registration numbers on these buses was surely no coincidence but was not repeated until 1961, after which it became standard practice. *John May*

No completely new double-deckers were bought after the last Leyland PD2s in 1953 until the first Atlanteans in 1959. Instead, large numbers of Tiger Cubs were ordered which in turn released some of the Leyland PS1s of 1947-49 for rebuilding as double-deckers. The PS1 chassis were stripped, upgraded and new Roe bodies fitted, thereby creating 35 'new' buses between 1955 and 1957. For a Roe body, they had an unfamiliar look, using a Park Royal steel frame rather than Roe's more usual teak frame. 1039 was one of the earliest conversions, back in service as a double-decker by the spring of 1955. It is pictured at Waterdale, Doncaster. *Geoff Warnes*

The rebuilt PS1s were given new registration numbers, the Barnsley Motor Tax Office taking a less strict view of what constituted a new vehicle. 1087, rebuilt and rebodied in 1957, is shown on Stand 14 in Barnsley Bus Station, picking up for Park House Estate. The rear of similar bus 1050, rebuilt in 1956, is visible alongside. Both were newly repainted when this picture was taken, the repaint including maroon mudguards introduced at the end of the 1950s, a change from the previous black. *Ken Jubb*

Willowbrook built the bodies for 24 Leyland Tiger Cubs in 1956/57, twelve each year (1059-1070 and 1093-1104). This 1957 example was new as 1100 but was photographed after the renumbering scheme of 1967, when it became 434 in the block allocated to short underfloor-engined single-deckers. It is approaching Doncaster's Southern Bus Station, having travelled through Hoyland, Wath, Mexborough and High Melton on its service 21 journey from High Green. *Ken Jubb collection*

1958 brought another 23 Leyland Tiger Cubs (1105-1127), this time with bodywork by Park Royal. When new they carried this mainly cream livery, considered more suitable for the first line of back-up for the coach fleet, which became extremely stretched over peak summer weekends. In March 1959 number 1122 stands in the centre of Barnsley Bus Station with its blinds set for trans-Pennine service 20 to Manchester via Penistone and Woodhead. In the background Camplejohn's Burlingham-bodied Atkinson awaits departure. *Geoffrey Morant*

The 1959 intake of 17 Tiger Cubs (1128-1144) had Willowbrook bodies to the BET's updated standard design, which had a more angular frontal appearance. On 25 October 1969, 467 (originally 1133) was working from Rawmarsh depot, taken over as part of the Mexborough & Swinton company at the start of the month, on former Mexborough & Swinton service 5 from Conisbrough and Mexborough to Rotherham. This picture shows it at Swinton Bridge over the Dearne & Dove Canal, with the Canal Tavern on the left and the Ship Inn on the right. *Geoff Warnes*

Rear-engined buses appeared in the fleet in December 1959, when twelve Leyland Atlanteans with Weymann lowbridge bodywork entered service. Numbered 1151-1162 they were the first completely new double-deckers for six years. 1158, displaying the L-suffix to indicate its low overall height, was photographed on a rural part of the journey from Doncaster to Barnsley on service 11. The route via Brodsworth, Hooton Pagnell, South Elmsall, Grimethorpe and Cudworth was the most northerly of several services between the two towns, passing numerous collieries but with attractive stretches of countryside interspersed. *Michael Fowler*

Waterdale in Doncaster was used as a coach departure point and a layover area for buses using the nearby bus station at Glasgow Paddocks and the terminus at North Bridge. Leyland Tiger Cub 1166 with Metro-Cammell bodywork was one of 23 delivered in 1960/61 (1163-1185) some of which, like 1166, were in the mainly cream coach livery, despite having bus-style seating. The rebuilt Tiger on the right, 1038, has the upper part of its radiator painted red and an oval Yorkshire Traction badge in place of the Leyland badge on the bus on the left. *Geoff Warnes*

By the end of 1960 the fleet was close to becoming 100% Leyland – the only exceptions were the Dennis Lancet buses and two Beadle-Commer buses. On 1 January 1961, the business of Camplejohn Brothers of Darfield was acquired and, remarkably, their four-strong bus fleet was retained and repainted into fleet colours. Three were Sentinels, including 130C (C for Camplejohn), an STC6 model that Camplejohn had bought new in 1952, and the fourth was an Atkinson. Six months after the takeover, in June 1961, 130C was photographed at Glasgow Paddocks ready for the 20-mile journey via Conisbrough, Mexborough, Wath and Wombwell to Barnsley on service 22A – a longer and more arduous run than it was used to with Camplejohn. *Geoff Warnes*

After an interval of several years, during which many single-deckers were rebuilt and the first Leyland Atlanteans arrived, 1961 saw a return to Leyland Titans. Numbers 1195-1205 were PD3s with the so-called St Helens-style fibreglass front and Northern Counties forward-entrance bodies with sliding doors. More followed in 1962 and 1964. Number 1200 was photographed at Glasgow Paddocks on 12 July 1961, when almost brand new. Behind it and ready to duplicate the service bus as far as Denaby, is a 1950 PD2, 881, with Roe lowbridge body. *Roger Holmes*

In 1960/61 another nine double-deck conversions were carried out, this time using Yorkshire Traction's seven PS2 chassis (the solitary bus and six that had carried Windover coach bodies) plus two from County Motors. The four done in 1960 had forward-entrance Northern Counties bodies, while the 1961 batch of five were by Roe, again with Park Royal steel frames. Roe-bodied 787 (originally 1191) is pictured in October 1969 – the non-standard livery with the cream band below the upper-deck windows was an attempt to improve their top-heavy appearance. The bus is in Barnsley town centre, heading for the bus station on service 111 from Athersley North, followed by number 199, a Bedford SB5 coach acquired with the business of Pickerill of Low Valley in 1964. *Geoffrey Morant*

The final Tiger Cubs were six with BET-style Alexander bodies (1212-1217) new in early 1962 (one is visible in the picture of Royal Tiger 998). Number 1212 proved to be ill-fated and in June 1967 its body was destroyed by fire in Barnsley Bus Station. It returned to service in 1968 with a new Alexander Y-type body as shown here, only to be withdrawn six years later after a collision. In this April 1972 picture and by then renumbered 502, it was waiting in Barnsley Bus Station for a journey to Manchester via Penistone and the Woodhead Pass. An X prefix had been added to what been service 20. *Omnibus Society/Peter Henson*

The O.600-engined Leyland Leopard was a welcome successor to the Tiger Cub. Early deliveries, in 1962, included three (1230-32) with Willowbrook bus-style bodies fitted out as coaches for use on long-distance express services. Renumbered 200-202 in 1967, in 1969 they were relegated to bus work, fitted with 53 bus seats, repainted into red bus livery and renumbered for a second time, to 343-345. The original side mouldings were kept but the frontal appearance was altered, with a new roof-mounted indicator box replacing the two apertures below the windscreen that had sufficed during their spell as coaches. In October 1969 343 was photographed in Pond Hill, Sheffield, having just left the Central Bus Station, with blinds set for the long service 70 from Upton, jointly operated with Sheffield. *Geoffrey Morant*

The double-deck conversion programme was completed in 1963 when nine more Tiger PS2 chassis were fitted with Northern Counties bodies of the same style as the first quartet in 1960. The chassis came from Yorkshire Woollen District as *Tracky* had no more of its own to use. 796 (previously 1245) is pictured in Barnsley Bus Station between journeys on the busy town services serving the Athersley and Kendray estates. Unlike the PD3s, the PS2 rebuilds all had conventional folding doors. The picture was taken in May 1969. *Omnibus Society/Roy Marshall*

Along with a second batch of lowbridge Atlanteans, 12 more Leyland PD3s with Northern Counties bodies came in 1964 (1276-1287). In this picture 727 (originally 1280), has just arrived in Barnsley Bus station for a brief stopover on the linked services from Carlton to Worsbrough Dale. The cross-town services were not advertised as such but the blind display gave a clue that the incoming bus from Carlton on service 85 would continue on the old tramway route to Worsbrough Dale (as service 57). The picture illustrates the somewhat awkward access to and from the cab. *Barry Ridge*

Opposite top The final ten Leyland Titans arrived in 1965; 1316-1325 were more forward-entrance PD3s but with Roe bodywork on Park Royal frames. In February 1971 743 (previously 1314) stands in Barnsley Bus Station, bound for Park House Estate. Fortunately most passengers knew their way round a system that could be confusing – service 106 ran to Athersley and service 102 to Park House but timetables referred to Park House as Kendray and failed to mention that the services were operationally linked. Previously the company had bought Atlanteans only when low-height buses were needed but after 1965 all new double-deckers were rear-engined. At the end of 1965 long-serving and popular general manager Norman Dean retired after 26 years; over the next few years none of his successors stayed nearly as long. *Omnibus Society/ Peter Henson*

Opposite Each year from 1962 to 1966 a batch of 36-foot long Leyland Leopards with typical BET-style bus-specification bodies was received. Most were 53-seaters but the 1962 batch had one extra seat. In total there were 43, most with Willowbrook bodies but the six 1964 buses were bodied by Marshall and the nine (1316-1324) that came in 1966 by Weymann. Weymann-bodied 342 (previously 1324), is passing along Blonk Street, Sheffield, with Samuel Osborn's Clyde Steel and Iron Works as a backdrop, at the end of the two-hour journey from Upton on service 70.

Geoffrey Morant

The original sequential fleet numbering series ended in 1966 with Atlanteans 1334-1343. They had the PDR1/2 chassis which, coupled with the stylish Northern Counties body, offered a bus of low overall height with a central upstairs gangway. In early 1967 the whole fleet was renumbered, separating different vehicle types into blocks, and what had been 1337 became 621 in a series starting at 600 for low-height rear-engined double-deckers. At the same time a new font was introduced for fleetnames and numbers, applied in cream instead of the previous gold. In August 1970 621 is seen in Central Bus Station, Leeds, working the former Burrows service from Rawmarsh, which was numbered 99 for as long as it remained intact under new ownership. *Omnibus Society/Peter Henson*

The Leyland Leopard met all single-deck needs and was bought in a variety of guises, for either coach or bus duties, but the 12 Marshall-bodied vehicles of 1967 (numbered 210-221) were the first true dual-purpose vehicles, equally at home in either role. They were ideally suited to the arduous trans-Pennine routes, with much more power than the Tiger Cubs that had preceded them and a more useful 49-seat capacity. This picture shows one-man-operated 218 leaving Lower Mosley Street bus station, Manchester, on service 20. *Malcolm King*

The twelve 1967 Atlanteans, 628-639, were striking buses featuring long panoramic windows in their Northern Counties bodies and were the first new double-deckers numbered under the new system. 638 is picture leaving Doncaster's Northern Bus Station in October 1969 on service 49 to Sprotbrough (mistakenly spelled with an extra 'o' on the blind), by now converted for driver-only operation with an Almex ticket machine – *Tracky* was an early user of this Swedish equipment. One of Doncaster's Leyland Royal Tiger Cubs follows on the Skellow service. *Geoffrey Morant*

The Alexander Y-type first appeared in the fleet in 1968 with three new Leyland Leopards (222-224) and the rebodied Tiger Cub shown in a previous picture. Further Leopards with Y-type bodies, all dual-purpose 49-seaters, followed at intervals until 1974, by which time they were delivered in NBC livery. 224 was one of the initial trio from 1968 and is pictured in May 1969 in Barnsley Bus Station, working service 42 to Ryhill. This was always a single-deck operation because of the low railway bridge adjacent to the former Royston & Notton Station. *Omnibus Society/Roy Marshall*

10

Pictured here in October 1969 soon after entering service, 662 was a Daimler Fleetline with Northern Counties bodywork. The first major departure from the policy of buying exclusively Leylands had been in 1968 when the double-deck order was split equally between Fleetlines and Atlanteans, with seven of each, and the 1969 order was the same. The bodywork was similar on both types and with no manufacturers' badges it was not easy to tell which was which. The bus is heading towards Barnsley Bus Station, on the local service to Worsbrough Common, a large housing estate built on a hillside south of the town. Rather unhelpfully the number blind displays only the letter A. *Geoffrey Morant*

Unusual deliveries in 1969 were four Willowbrook-bodied Atlantean PDR1A/1s, 747-750, which had been destined for Devon General and were used for a couple of years in the latter's livery, as in this picture. Number 750 was to have been Devon General 545 (OTT 545G) but was instead allocated a Barnsley registration. These buses were taller than the other Atlanteans in the fleet and were numbered in the series for full-height buses. In this October 1969 photograph it is leaving Barnsley Bus Station on service 65 to Sheffield; in effect a short-working of the lengthy through services to Sheffield – 66 from Bradford via Dewsbury and 67 from Leeds via Wakefield, which came together in Barnsley. The 66 and 67 were later replaced by the White Rose Express services via the M1 motorway – as the slogan 'all the way by motorway' on the side of the bus indicates, the M1 had already transformed the Yorkshire Services to London. *Omnibus Society/Peter Henson*

County Motors of Lepton had been jointly owned by Yorkshire Traction, Yorkshire Woollen and West Riding and with the latter passing into National Bus Company control, was absorbed by Yorkshire Traction at the start of 1969. The fleet included four Guy Arab IVs with Roe lowbridge bodywork (County's double-deck buying policy had generally followed West Riding's and even extended to two Wulfrunians which were soon moved to West Riding's fleet). Surprisingly the four Arabs were repainted red and placed in service from Barnsley depot, where their rear platform doors were a

unique feature. 685 was working the Higham service acquired from Mosley's in 1965 and is seen in September 1970 in Eldon Street, passing the stone abutments of the bridge that had carried the railway into the now-closed Court House station. *Malcolm King*

County Motors' single-deck fleet had followed BET-group policies and the takeover brought with it 11 Leopards. 390 was one of the earliest pair, Willowbrook-bodied 54-seaters dating from 1962, with Willowbrook's distinctive frontal trim. On 17 July 1971 in Lord Street, Huddersfield, it awaits departure for Barnsley on service 32, the former County operation to Barnsley via Grange Moor, Flockton and Bretton. It had been converted for one-man operation by County and still has their fold-over style of indicator rather than an illuminated sign. *Omnibus Society/Roy Marshall*

Six Tiger Cubs, a model last bought by Yorkshire Traction in 1962, were also transferred with the County business, including a pair of late models with Marshall bodies new in 1967/68. 598 (former County 113) had migrated to Barnsley depot and is pictured working as a one-man bus on the shortest local service in the town, the four-minute run to Rockingham Street on service 91. *Barry Ridge*

Further National Bus Company rationalisation later in 1969 resulted in Mexborough & Swinton being absorbed on 1 October. This brought even more variety into the fleet, although most non-standard types did not last long. Northern Counties-bodied Daimler Fleetline 699 had been Mexborough 25, new the previous year. In this view it still displays the former Mexborough & Swinton service number as it heads along the Inner Relief Road in Mexborough in May 1970 on its way from Conisbrough to the Drill Hall terminus at Highwoods, on the other side of Mexborough town centre. *Omnibus Society/Peter Henson*

At the time of the takeover Mexborough & Swinton had three single-deck Daimler Fleetlines with Marshall dual-purpose bodies on order – which would have been their first new single-deckers for a decade – primarily intended for Mexborough's share of the White Rose Express services which used the newly extended M1 motorway. They were delivered in 1970 to *Tracky* as 228-230. Number 230 was only a few weeks old when photographed in Leeds in July 1970, bound for Mexborough via Rotherham on what would have been a Mexborough & Swinton operation, service X35. In the event the Y-type Leopards proved far more suitable for the job and in 1972 the three Fleetlines were demoted to bus use and renumbered 541-543. *Omnibus Society/Roy Marshall*

Further bus-bodied Leopards arrived in 1970 – a batch of eleven with Willowbrook bodies (346-356). 354 is pictured here in May 1971 pulling out of Barnsley Bus Station for a service 23 journey to Thurnscoe (Whinwood Estate) via Wombwell and Wath. Although equipped for one-man operation a conductor was carried on this busy service. *Omnibus Society/Peter Henson*

The winding-up of the Sheffield Joint Omnibus Committee had some unexpected consequences, Five Park Royal-bodied Daimler Fleetlines were on order for the Sheffield C fleet but were instead delivered to Yorkshire Traction as 752-756. The bodies did not have Sheffield's peaked dome at front and back but did have the Sheffield-style front bumper and the outline of the Sheffield front destination indicator box. They were based at Barnsley depot and in June 1971 number 754 was photographed leaving the bus station on the short run to Rockingham Street at Smithies; it was scheduled to return nine minutes later, after a minute's layover at the outer terminus. These buses marked the end of an era as *Tracky*'s next double-deckers, two years later, were Bristol VRs in National Bus Company livery. *Omnibus Society/Peter Henson*

Opposite top The balance of the single-deck bus order for 1970 was the company's only foray into a more contemporary design of urban single-decker with styled front end, sloping window pillars, rear engine and dual doorways. There were nine of these Alexander-bodied Daimler Fleetlines (357-365) but they were not considered a success and remained the only rear-engined single-deckers until the era of the ubiquitous Leyland National. 365 pulls out of Doncaster's Northern Bus Station, bound for Upton (Rose Estate) via Adwick-le-Street and Skellow in June 1971. *Geoffrey Morant*

Opposite In 1972 the fleet got its final Leyland Leopard buses – thirteen 53-seaters (372-384) and 12 shorter 45-seaters (529-540), all with Marshall bodywork. Number 384 epitomises this last generation of robust underfloor-engined single-deckers as it arrives at Sheffield's Central Bus Station on service 70. Until the acquisition of Mexborough & Swinton and the introduction of the White Rose Express services, all *Tracky* buses from Sheffield first ran north to Chapeltown, where the services split, running either to Penistone, Huddersfield and later Halifax (service 68), to Barnsley and beyond (65-67) or to Wombwell and Upton (70). The picture was taken in March 1972, two months after 384 had entered service. *Omnibus Society/Peter Henson*

Mexborough & Swinton

There were a few quirky operators in the BET portfolio and one of the quirkiest was the Mexborough & Swinton Tramways Company Ltd ("M&S"), whose main operating territory lay to the north of Rotherham, following the course of the River Don as far as Conisbrough.

It began as a tramway operator in 1907, with a 6½-mile line built by the National Electric Construction Company from Rotherham through Rawmarsh and Swinton to Mexborough. Trolleybuses were introduced in 1915 on short services feeding into the tramway but up to 1924 only seven had been acquired and operations were halted for lengthy periods. In the meantime, a regular motor bus service between Mexborough and Goldthorpe started in 1922.

Big changes came in 1928/29, with a new fleet of trolleybuses replacing the trams and the earlier trolleybuses. The main service from Rotherham was extended to Brook Square at Conisbrough, while a second service ran between Manvers Main and a terminus at Conanby (referred to as Conisbrough High). An Act of Parliament protected the trolleybuses from competition but a formal agreement covering operating rights in the Mexborough, Swinton and Conisbrough areas was made with Yorkshire Traction and the Goldthorpe service was handed over to the latter.

Traction replaced Tramways in the company name and for the next thirty years Mexborough & Swinton was primarily a trolleybus operator, notable for its unusual all-single-deck fleet. The BET Group took control of operations from the NECC in 1931 and the network remained stable with only a couple of minor extensions in Mexborough and Rawmarsh. Between 1943 and 1950 thirty-nine new Sunbeam trolleybuses replaced all remaining pre-war models, which included some second-hand acquisitions, and a green livery replaced the previous maroon.

By the 1950s it was clear that motor buses were better suited to cater for the new housing developments on either side of the core trolleybus route and ten Leyland Tiger Cubs were ordered. Arriving in 1954, they took the motor bus fleet into double figures for the first time, enabling new services to begin and also the first trolleybus conversion. More Tiger Cubs followed, including some crush loaders with reduced seating and extra standing room, intended to meet the demand for short journeys at colliery shift times. It was then inevitable that the trolleybus system would close – it was the BET Group's last – and the necessary approval was secured in 1960. The changeover took place in two stages in early 1961, with low-height Leyland Atlantean double-deckers taking over the trunk route to Conisbrough and Tiger Cubs providing the Manvers service, which still had to be single-deck operated.

Despite BET Group ownership, the company was run entirely separately from neighbouring Yorkshire Traction and until the late 1960s there were no jointly-operated services, although it provided occasional duplicates on Yorkshire Traction's busy Doncaster – Kilnhurst service.

By contrast, operations were heavily entwined with those of Rotherham Corporation, which shared the main route from Rotherham to Mexborough and Conisbrough, successively using trams, trolleybuses and motor buses. During the 1960s second-hand buses and coaches were drafted in from within the BET Group – the prime source was Brighton-based Southdown, a factor being that its green livery saved the cost of a repaint.

In the late 1960s some management functions were combined with those of Yorkshire Traction but it was only after the creation of the National Bus Company in January 1969 that the company's future was really threatened. The end came after just nine months, when the company was integrated into Yorkshire Traction, which continued to use the Rawmarsh depot, although the smaller one at the Old Toll Bar, which dated back to tramway days, was closed in 1968.

Mexborough town centre was at the heart of the trolleybus system and this is the important junction of High Street, Main Street and Swinton Road. Sunbeam W 31 is heading south towards Swinton and Rotherham on service A from Adwick Road, the Leyland Tiger Cub in the background is facing towards Conisbrough and the trolleybus wires to the left, in front of the Post Office, lead off towards Manvers Main. The fleet is in transition, with the Sunbeam representing the old order and the Tiger Cub the new. Although everything looks normal, this is 25 March 1961, the penultimate day of scheduled trolleybus operation. *Geoff Warnes*

Post-war fleet renewal began in 1947 with 18 new Sunbeams, numbered 7-24 to follow on from six utility trolleybuses (1-6) delivered in 1943. Like the wartime buses, they were Sunbeam Ws with centre-entrance bodywork by Brush but with a more rounded outline. Twelve similar buses (25-36) came in 1948 – they were F4 models with slightly more powerful motors. In June 1955 Sunbeam W 7 heads towards Mexborough and Manvers Main whilst F4 number 25 travels the other way to Conisbrough High (the company's designation for the Conanby terminus), both on service C. Number 31, another 1948 bus, is following. The photograph was taken from a favourite vantage point, the footbridge over the main Sheffield to Doncaster railway line at Denaby level crossing. The crossing was a cause of frequent delays to the trolleybus service. *Geoff Warnes*

The final trolleybuses (37-39), again Brush-bodied Sunbeam F4s, arrived in the summer of 1950, bringing the post-war fleet to 33 and ousting the last pre-war trolleybuses. This is 37 showing service letter C on both blinds and Manvers Main as its destination. Wath also gets a mention, although the town centre was nearly a mile from the Manvers terminus. Despite the blind display the bus is actually travelling along Wath Road away from the Manvers complex, which provides the industrial backdrop. The railway lines on the right curve away towards Bolton-on-Dearne and those on the left lead towards Wath North and Cudworth. 15 of the Sunbeams went on to have afterlives as double-deckers with Yorkshire municipal operators; eight sold in the 1950s to Doncaster were rebodied with new Roe rear-entrance bodies. Number 37 was one of seven F4s that survived to the end of the system and were then bought by Bradford and fitted with new forward-entrance East Lancs bodies. *Geoff Warnes*

In complete contrast to so much of the system, industry is completely absent from this scene showing 35 heading along Low Road towards the Conisbrough Low terminus at Brook Square. Towering above the trolleybus is the 12th-century keep of Conisbrough Castle, one of South Yorkshire's most famous landmarks. Operation of service B from Rotherham to Conisbrough Low was shared with Rotherham (which referred to it as service 9), whereas the Conisbrough High service C was run exclusively by Mexborough & Swinton; this followed several steep and narrow roads on the far side of the castle as it ascended to Conisbrough town centre and the terminus at Conanby. *Geoff Warnes*

This is the scene at the Brook Square (Conisbrough Low) terminus on 26 March 1961, the final day of normal trolleybus operation. 35 will negotiate the turning circle to return to Rotherham on service B, behind it on Doncaster Road are Rotherham Corporation 3 and Mexborough 39. Following the trolleybuses is one of Yorkshire Traction's first batch of Leyland Atlanteans, working service 22 from Barnsley to Doncaster. *Geoff Warnes*

Until 1954 the majority of mileage had been operated by the trolleybuses but the fleet also included a few motor buses and coaches. In 1952 four pre-war AEC Regals from Devon General replaced some early post-war Bedford OBs but more significant change began when ten Leyland Tiger Cubs (40-49) arrived in 1954. Four replaced the Regals while the others allowed the conversion of the Green Lane trolleybus service to motor buses. The new buses had standard BET-design Weymann bodies; two were later given more comfortable seating and repainted in a mainly cream livery in order to back up the small coach fleet. In this form number 40 is seen in Rotherham Bus Station awaiting departure for Upper Haugh.
Omnibus Society

In 1946 T P O'Donnell was appointed to manage the company, having previously served as a trolleybus engineer with London Transport; in 1954 he moved on to become general manager with another trolleybus operator, Ashton-under-Lyne Corporation. His successor, D R Vernon, was recruited from within BET, coming from Maidstone & District. He introduced high-capacity Leyland Tiger Cubs to cater for short-distance peak loadings. The first pair (50/51) entered service early in 1957 and could carry 61 passengers, only 32 of them seated; to achieve this there were six single seats on the nearside and two on the offside, while an extended front overhang allowed a wider entrance than usual. They were put to use on new service D, which strengthened the Manvers to Conisbrough High trolleybus service and also diverted into the Windhill Estate in Mexborough, continuing at the Conisbrough end to Ellershaw. 51 is pictured loading for Ellershaw in Bank Street, Mexborough. *Geoffrey Morant*

Number 54 was the only fleet addition in 1959, a 41-seat Weymann-bodied Leyland Tiger Cub with a more conventional layout than the standee buses of the preceding two years. The company's buses reached Sheffield in February 1965 when service 90 was introduced in response to the Sheffield – Rotherham – Thurnscoe service started by Dearneways in October 1964. Dearneways' application was seen by the established operators as an invasion of their territory that could not be left unchallenged; the result was this limited-stop service from Sheffield to Mexborough, jointly licensed with Rotherham Corporation and Sheffield JOC but operated solely by Mexborough & Swinton. It was the company's longest service and initially had eight round trips, leaving Windhill at Mexborough every two hours from 7.32 am to 9.32 pm. Crew-operated 54 is shown here in August 1967 in Pond Hill, Sheffield, having just left the Central Bus Station. *Geoffrey Morant*

The decision to replace the single-deck trolleybuses with Leyland Atlanteans was a radical move – with 72 seats each bus had more than double the seating capacity of a trolleybus. Initially it was calculated that only eleven would be needed but three more arrived in 1961/62, all with similar Weymann lowbridge bodywork. Their frontal appearance was enhanced by the moulding below the windscreen of the style used by Maidstone & District on its similar vehicles. Notably they had Leyland O.680 engines, more powerful than the O.600 usually fitted to Atlanteans at that time. The last of the first order, number 11, is pictured in May 1967 in Rotherham Bus Station with a particularly comprehensive destination display for the Rawmarsh circular service. It had recently been repainted with the fleetname repositioned to the front of the upper-deck side panels and a prominent front advertisement for the Mexborough-based South Yorkshire Times. *Ken Jubb*

With twelve modern Leyland Atlanteans in stock by mid-1961, the next double-deckers could hardly have been a greater contrast – two 1939 Leyland Titan TD5s acquired from Southdown. How many other operators ran Atlanteans before getting their first front-engined double-decker? The Northern Counties bodies were only half the age of the chassis, which went some way towards concealing their lengthy past, but the black exhaust smoke as 16 pulls away from Frederick Street, Rotherham on 22 September 1962 tells its own tale. It was working service 8, the former trolleybus service A – use of service letters ceased with the end of the trolleybuses. The TD5s did not last long and a replacement number 16 had arrived by early 1963, also from Southdown. Noted for its high maintenance standards, Southdown supplied all the front-engined double-deckers operated by Mexborough & Swinton. *Geoff Warnes*

The Leyland Tiger Cubs and Atlanteans had their entrances beside the driver and the acquired Leyland Titans reintroduced a way of working for the crews that had disappeared with the trolleybuses. It was said that some conductors and drivers disliked working together so the arrival of the elderly Titans actually suited some of them, if not the passengers. Another likely reason for selecting Southdown as a source was that the buses could be put into service in the latter's green livery without looking out of place. 16's rear blind indicates its use on the busy service 9A to Conisbrough as it heads out of Rotherham under corporation trolleybus wires and past the roundabout being constructed at the junction of Frederick Street and Effingham Street. *Tony Belton*

113

In the spring of 1963 four more Leyland Titans were acquired from Southdown to expand the double-deck fleet, although one of them was not used. These were 1946 PD1s with Park Royal bodies and were older than the now-withdrawn post-war trolleybus fleet. They were repainted into M&S's green and cream instead of retaining Southdown livery and had their seating capacity increased from 54 to 58. Clearly visible is the extended fleetname style introduced after the withdrawal of the trolleybuses. It included the Swinton element of the company title; the trolleybuses had always shown plain Mexborough. In May 1963, 18 heads for Rotherham past the South Yorkshire Hotel in Swinton Road, Mexborough. *Geoff Warnes*

More Southdown Leyland Titans came north in 1964, this time a pair of 1948 PD2/1s with Leyland bodies. They lasted until 1967 and in May of that year 17 was photographed leaving the recently opened Rotherham Bus Station for Conisbrough on service 9. In the background, working the much shorter service 6 to Manor Farm, is Midland Red 6048, an Alexander-bodied Daimler Fleetline borrowed by Mexborough & Swinton for evaluation purposes. *Ken Jubb*

It was not only double-deckers that came from Southdown; between 1962 and 1965 eight coaches were acquired from the same source, all with centre-entrances. The first three were Beadle rebuilds based on pre-war Leyland Tigers, while the others were Royal Tigers. Southdown coaches were painted in two shades of green, quite different from the company's bus livery; because of this, the acquired vehicles were all smartly repainted into Mexborough & Swinton's mainly cream coach livery. Number 107 was one of a pair with Leyland coachwork acquired in late 1963. Two identical vehicles arrived a year later. *Ken Jubb*

The last coach to come from Southdown was this Leyland Royal Tiger with Harrington Wayfarer coachwork, specially built to a reduced width of 7ft 6in for use on tours of Ireland. It dated from 1955 and was acquired ten years later, putting in three years' service in its new home. Numbered 103 and eminently suitable for use on private hires, it was photographed on the forecourt of Rawmarsh depot, displaying the abbreviated Mexborough fleetname, unlike 107 above, which has the full version. *Ken Jubb*

From the 1950s the company sought to develop a high quality coach operation and two Leyland Tiger Cubs with Burlingham Seagull bodies were bought, one in 1955, the other in 1958. Following the delivery of three new Leyland Leopard coaches in 1965-67, they were relegated to bus duties and converted for one-man-operation. 101, the newer of the pair, retained much of its original appearance when photographed in Sheaf Street, Sheffield, at the end of a journey from Mexborough on service 90, with its Pay on Entry sign displayed. *Malcolm King*

Until 1964 all double-deckers had been Leylands but a single Daimler Fleetline with Weymann bodywork broke the mould. One of the attractions of the Fleetline chassis was that it allowed a low overall height body with a central-gangway layout and all subsequent new double-deckers were Fleetlines with Gardner engines. It was the last bus to have the Maidstone & District style moulding on the front panel. Interestingly, Maidstone & District also switched from Atlanteans to Fleetlines at about the same time. This view shows the bus, number 19, when new at Windmill Avenue in Conisbrough – referred to as 'Conisborough W' on the destination blind (on which it is wrongly spelled with an extra 'o'). *Michael Fowler*

D R Vernon moved to become general manager of Yorkshire Woollen in 1966 and his successor at Mexborough was A J Price. No more second-hand double-deckers were acquired and the only new ones were ten 1967/68 Daimler Fleetlines with Northern Counties bodies. They were numbered 15-18 and 20-25, fitting around the original Fleetline. After little over a year the first four were transferred to West Riding in early 1969 in one of the earliest of such moves within the newly formed National Bus Company. West Riding had exceptional needs as a result of problems with its fleet of Guy Wulfrunians. In December 1967, immediately after entering service, 15 was photographed in Kilnhurst Road while working Rawmarsh Circular service 7, with the spoil heaps of Kilnhurst Colliery in the distance. *Michael Fowler*

Probably the most remarkable second-hand acquisitions of the 1960s were two Bedford SBs with Yeates Pegasus bodies. They had previously run for independents and were bought second-hand in early 1968, an exceptional move for a BET company. 115 came from Reliance of Stainforth and was initially placed in service as a one-man bus in Reliance's two-tone blue livery. Later it was repainted into green and cream, as it was here in Rotherham Bus Station, apparently on a short working of service 6 back to Rawmarsh depot. The pair lasted long enough to pass to Yorkshire Traction, which soon sold them to Baddeley Brothers at Holmfirth. *Omnibus Society/Peter Henson*

The modified Burlingham Seagull coaches, now relegated to use as one-man buses, were among the forty vehicles passed to Yorkshire Traction in October 1969 when Mexborough & Swinton was merged into its larger neighbour. The older of the pair, 100, had undergone a thorough rebuild, losing the majority of its trim. It became Yorkshire Traction 191 and is shown here, in the month of takeover, incongruously carrying the red script Yorkshire Traction coach-style fleetname. The location is Rotherham Bus Station and the bus is on service 4 to Manor Farm, while the Leyland Atlantean behind, formerly Mexborough & Swinton 14 but now Yorkshire Traction 693, is on service 6 to Rawmarsh. *Geoffrey Morant*

The Barnsley Independents

BURROWS · CAMPLEJOHN · IDEAL (TAYLOR) · IDEAL (WRAY) · MOSLEY · LARRATT PEPPER · ROWE

In the 1920s and 1930s the Barnsley area was awash with small independent bus operators. Many ran only one or two buses and most succumbed to Yorkshire Traction's expansionist advances, especially during the 1930s. The survivors were forced to accept a particular niche in the market and by the 1950s the remaining independents were each confined to a single service, sometimes supplemented by a few colliery or works journeys. None provided really frequent services, running hourly at best. Significantly though, all were granted access to Yorkshire Traction's bus station – in fact every bus service in Barnsley used it and buses from at least fifteen operators could be seen there. No wonder it was a popular spot for photographers.

In the 1960s Yorkshire Traction renewed its drive to establish a near-monopoly and one by one most of the surviving independent stage-carriage services were picked off. Camplejohn of Darfield ceased theirs at the end of 1960, Mosley of Barugh Green followed in 1965, Burrows of Wombwell in 1966, Taylor (Ideal) of Cudworth in 1967 and Rowe of Cudworth in 1969. Only Wray of Hoyle Mill, the other half of the Ideal partnership, and Larratt Pepper of Thurnscoe continued to run stage-carriage services into the 1970s, although some of the others remained in business as coach operators after giving up their bus services.

Two smaller operators, Smith of Darfield and Pickerill of Low Valley, also lasted into the 1960s, working the short local link between Darfield and Wombwell; they tended to use small coaches on their services and are not featured here.

Burrows' service from Rawmarsh to Leeds was an impressive operation and profitable enough to justify new double-deckers. It was by far the longest of the independents' services and unique in running across Barnsley (via Doncaster Road and Wakefield Road), rather than terminating in the town.

Doncaster Road was also used by Camplejohn and Larratt Pepper on their services from Thurnscoe but both stuck to single-deckers. Pontefract Road saw the greatest concentration of independent activity, with three independents and Yorkshire Traction all running Barnsley – Pontefract services. South Yorkshire Motors (fully covered in *The Colours of West Yorkshire* because, despite the name, its base was in Pontefract) and Yorkshire Traction shared the more direct service via Ackworth, while Taylor and Wray ran via South Elmsall, under the shared Ideal Service title. Also competing for business through Cudworth was Arthur Rowe, whose service branched off at Shafton to reach Carlton and Royston. By the late 1950s all five operators were running double-deckers, the railway bridge at Cudworth dictating that they were of lowbridge configuration.

Mosley's was different on two counts. Since 1952 their service to Higham along Huddersfield Road had been the only independent presence west of Barnsley town centre, the cream and green livery ensuring that their buses stood out from the crowd. Curiously, all the other operators illustrated here used varying shades of red and cream, giving the impression that they wanted to blend in with each other and with Yorkshire Traction rather than proclaim their independence.

T Burrows & Sons

T (Tommy) Burrows & Sons operated one of the longest independent stage-carriage services in Yorkshire, linking Rawmarsh and Leeds via Wombwell, Barnsley and Wakefield. The round trip of around 75 miles took five hours and from the late 1940s most trips were double-deck operated, often requiring a duplicate bus for at least part of the way. The first double-deckers were two Strachans-bodied Bristol K6As allocated by the government in 1945. Number 50 was one of them, rebodied in 1957 by Burlingham with an 8ft-wide body which had the added refinement of platform doors. In this June 1964 scene in Barnsley Bus Station it was heading north for Leeds as was the Yorkshire Traction double-deck rebodied Leyland PS1 behind, on service 67 from Sheffield. Both services ran hourly, and were co-ordinated to run every 30 minutes between Barnsley and Wakefield – apparently something had gone awry on this occasion. *Ken Jubb*

In 1953 five former London Transport double-deckers were acquired: two pre-war STL class AEC Regents and three wartime Daimler CWA6s. Between 1956 and 1958 the Daimlers were fitted with new Burlingham highbridge bodies, similar to that on Bristol 50, while two of four AEC Regents bought new in 1946/47 with Strachans lowbridge bodies were similarly dealt with by Roe. In this June 1964 picture, ex-London Daimler 81 is followed through the stalls of Barnsley's famous open market by 55, one of the Roe rebodied AEC Regents.
Iain MacGregor

Burrows' final double-deck purchases, in 1965, were four former Devon General AEC Regent IIIs with Weymann highbridge bodies dating from 1952. They were the first second-hand double-deckers since 1953. 104 looked superb in this view in Leeds Central Bus Station before the application of external adverts. In October 1966 the bus service was sold to Yorkshire Traction along with twelve double-deckers (these four, the six rebodies from the late 1950s and the Regents that Burrows had bought new in 1949 and 1956). None were used by their new owner and only two avoided immediate scrapping. Yorkshire Traction maintained the former Burrows service for a few years, licensed jointly with West Riding, allocating it the number 99, while Burrows continued with coaches and contract services until 1974; *Malcolm King*

Opposite top After an AEC Regent III in 1949 Burrows bought only one more new double-decker, an AEC Regent V supplied in 1956. Both had lowbridge bodywork by Roe. The later bus, 89, is about to leave Barnsley Bus Station on a Leeds to Rawmarsh journey, displaying the TBS fleetname rather than the company title. *Ken Jubb*

Opposite After the Regent V came two 1956 AEC Reliances with Burlingham bodies – the first single-deck service buses since a pair of Bedford OWBs in 1945. Number 90 was the first of the pair and replaced a 1936 AEC Regal. Double-deckers were still the mainstay of the service in September 1959 when the Reliance was photographed picking up in Barnsley Bus Station, bound for Rawmarsh. Notably, Yorkshire Traction allowed Burrows to use the same stand as some of their own buses to Wombwell – a level of co-ordination that might not have been expected. *Roger Holmes*

Camplejohn Brothers

Camplejohn Brothers were based at Darfield and operated a service between Thurnscoe and Barnsley until selling out to Yorkshire Traction at the end of 1960. In 1952 they acquired a pair of Sentinel STC6s, one a former demonstrator and this one which was bought new. They were the front-line service buses for a number of years and lasted to pass with the business to Yorkshire Traction, which used them for a couple of years in its otherwise almost exclusively Leyland fleet. This June 1959 view of 29 is at Camplejohn's depot. *Roger Holmes*

Opposite top In the mid-1950s the bus fleet was updated with two Burlingham-bodied 44-seaters, an Atkinson and a Sentinel, each of which had been displayed by its manufacturer at the 1954 Commercial Motor Show. This is 32, which had previously served as a demonstrator for Atkinson. Surprisingly, Yorkshire Traction took Camplejohn's four service buses (three Sentinels and the Atkinson) into its operational fleet, along with two equally non-standard coaches. This 1958 view shows the bus leaving Barnsley Bus Station with a healthy load on one of the direct journeys to Thurnscoe via Ardsley; alternate journeys took a less direct route via Wombwell and Low Valley. *Geoffrey Morant*

Opposite Camplejohn's 33 was 775 ERF, a Burlingham-bodied Sentinel SLC6/30, shown here in Barnsley bus station. Its first operator was Green Bus of Rugeley, Staffordshire, which used it for a couple of years before it came to Yorkshire late in 1955. The livery differs from the Atkinson, with a red roof, Camplejohn Bros title on a cream band above the windows and a darker red for the lower panels. The photograph was taken in July 1960. *John Kaye*

Ideal (Taylor)

The Ideal Service partnership was established in the 1920s. Originally there were five members but by the mid-1930s only two remained – Taylor and Wray who jointly operated an hourly service from Barnsley to Pontefract via Hemsworth, South Elmsall and Upton. Until the 1950s it was single-deck operated but both partners then acquired double-deckers. The first for R Taylor & Sons was YWT 572, which took to the road in 1959. It may have looked like a brand-new bus but was actually a new Roe body on a Leyland Tiger PS1 chassis which, as FWX 932, had previously carried a Wilks & Meade coach body. Wray had successfully undertaken a similar conversion in 1956. Taylor's only other double-decker was a former Ribble Leyland PD2 with Brush bodywork bought in 1966. In April 1967 the Taylors sold their share of the Ideal Service to Yorkshire Traction, both double-deckers passing to Wray. *Ken Jubb*

The Taylor fleet, which operated from premises at Cudworth, got its first underfloor-engined service bus in 1954, when a new Roe-bodied Leyland Royal Tiger replaced a pre-war Tiger. In 1957 it was joined by a Leyland Tiger Cub with Burlingham body, and the third and last was this 1952 Leyland Royal Tiger with Leyland bodywork, acquired in 1961 from Aberdeenshire operator Simpson of Rosehearty. All three survived to the end of Taylor's bus operations in 1967, when the Tiger Cub passed with the double-deckers to Wray. This Barnsley Bus Station view shows the Royal Tiger ready to pull on to the stand for a run to Pontefract, a journey scheduled to take one hour and twenty-five minutes. *Ken Jubb*

Ideal (Wray)

Wray was an earlier convert to double-deckers than his Ideal partner and after 1955 only bought double-deckers until acquiring Taylor's Leyland Tiger Cub in 1967. For many years second-hand Leyland Titans were popular (lowbridge, of necessity), and HJN 841 was a former Southend Corporation PD2 dating from 1954, acquired in 1966. In later years a darker shade of red was used, with varying amounts of cream relief. The photograph was taken at the Hoyle Mill premises in Barnsley, where most buses were kept in the open, and also shows the Leyland PS1 rebuild acquired from Taylor in 1967 and a former Ribble Leyland PD2. *Roger Holmes*

After acquiring many used Leyland Titans Wray developed a liking for Bristols, starting in 1969 with a rebodied wartime K5G. Later, four Bristol-engined Lodekkas were acquired, an unusual type for South Yorkshire, and the last bus to join the fleet, in late 1973, was a Dennis Loline III. Towards the end buses were usually placed into service in as-acquired condition as with OWX 164, one of three Lodekkas that had previously run for the West Yorkshire Road Car Company and were bought in 1971. It is shown leaving Pontefract for Barnsley in April 1972, displaying the service number 46 which Yorkshire Traction had allocated when it took over Taylor's share in 1967. Wray sold out at the end of March 1974, bringing the Ideal service to an end after half a century. *Geoffrey Morant*

J W Mosley & Sons

After 1952 J W Mosley & Sons of Barugh Green was the only independent bus operator on the west side of Barnsley; the service ran via Huddersfield Road to Barugh Green where it turned left up the hill to Higham. The village is barely three miles from Barnsley but was served only by Mosley after Barnsley & District withdrew their limited competing service in the 1920s. The first double-decker was a utility Guy Arab acquired from Birmingham in 1951; in 1954 it was replaced by this former Southport Corporation Duple-bodied Daimler CWA6, which put in almost six years' service at Barugh Green. This picture shows it at the depot in June 1959, with prominent, if unusual, painted advertisements. Larratt Pepper's Daimler Freeline is parked behind it. Among the visitors the Freeline had brought was Roy Marshall (on the right), who at the time was Southport Corporation's Traffic Superintendent. *Roger Holmes*

Opposite top Mosley's fourth double-decker was this 1945 Daimler CWD6, one of the three rebodied by Roe for the Sheffield Transport Department in 1953. Bought in 1960 to replace a Guy Arab that had also come from Sheffield. It is pictured leaving Barnsley Bus Station on a fine day in September 1964. A Northern General dual-purpose single-decker on express work is visible in the background. Mosley's sold the bus service to Yorkshire Traction in May 1965 but continued to run coaches from the Barugh Green garage well into the 1990s. *Ken Jubb*

Opposite The double-decker was often inadequate for the busy Higham service and a single-deck duplicate was frequently provided. This uncommon Guy Warrior with Meadows engine and Mulliner bodywork was bought in 1961 to fulfil these duties. It replaced a possibly even more unusual vehicle, a 1952 Tilling-Stevens with a Duple Vega coach-style body fitted with bus seating. UWW 769 dated from 1957 and had previously run for Blue Line of Armthorpe. It lacks any fleetname in this view in Barnsley Bus Station, but Mosley's cream and green livery ensured that it stood out from the Yorkshire Traction Leylands in the background. *Iain MacGregor*

Larratt Pepper

Larratt Pepper's stage carriage service from Thurnscoe to Barnsley via Great Houghton and Darfield was co-ordinated to an extent with the similar service operated by Camplejohn and with Yorkshire Traction timings, following their acquisition of McAdoo's service in 1940. Number 15 in the very varied fleet was this 1952 Daimler Freeline with Daimler engine and Burlingham body, bought primarily for use on the bus service but with 44 comfortable seats a useful back-up for the coach fleet. This 1959 view shows it with a typical semi-rural Dearne Valley backdrop, possibly about to begin its day's service. *Roger Holmes*

Larratt Pepper had a single Albion – this Plaxton Highway bodied Aberdonian, bought new in 1958 which remained in the fleet until 1973. Departures from Barnsley were scheduled at two-hourly intervals but duplicates were regularly provided and this picture shows number 19 preparing to operate the full route to Thurnscoe whilst Freeline 15 waits on the stand for a short journey to Darfield. The LP logo, displayed in place of a service number, is presented differently on each bus. *Ken Jubb*

The only 36ft-long buses in the fleet were a pair of Leyland Leopards with Plaxton Derwent bodies dating from 1969/70. They survived until the end of Pepper's bus-operating days in May 1978 but the sale to Yorkshire Traction did not include any of the buses. Number 34 was the later example, a 53-seater, and is shown on layover in Barnsley Bus Station before returning to Thurnscoe via Little Houghton, where buses turned near the entrance to Houghton Main Colliery in the course of a mile-long double-run from Middlecliffe. *Roy Marshall*

The last new bus to enter the fleet was 36, a 1971 Bedford YRQ which, like the Leopards of the previous two years, had a Plaxton Derwent body. It was a 49-seater, achieved by three-plus-two seating at the back of the saloon. This picture, taken at the company's premises in Thurnscoe, shows the clear and detailed destination blind featured on later buses. When Larratt Pepper sold the bus service (crew-operated to the end) number 36 passed to Arthur Rowe for contract work, Pepper continuing to run the coach business until the 1990s. *Malcolm King*

Arthur Rowe & Sons

Arthur Rowe & Sons operated an indirect Barnsley – Royston service, running via Pontefract Road through Cudworth to Shafton, where it turned sharp left by Yorkshire Traction's depot to reach Royston by way of Shaw Lane and Carlton. Only one bus was needed for the scheduled timetable and from the early 1950s it was often a double-decker. In the course of the decade two pre-war vehicles were acquired (an AEC Regent and a Leyland Titan), followed by five wartime models, four Guy Arabs and a Daimler CWA6, each from a different source. Guy Arab DCR 866 originated with Hants & Dorset where its wartime Roe body had been extensively rebuilt by Portsmouth Aviation; it had had a brief spell with Greyhound, Sheffield, before reaching Rowe in late 1956. Here it awaits departure from Barnsley Bus Station, where Rowe's bus appeared at two-hourly intervals. *Geoffrey Morant*

BRN 265 represented a huge improvement on the utility Guys and Daimlers that Rowe had previously operated. It was a former Ribble 'White Lady', with Burlingham body on a Leyland PD1/3 chassis, and was only eleven years old when acquired in 1959. Another similar bus joined the fleet in 1960. BRN 265 stands at the Ship Hotel terminus in Royston (so-named because of its proximity to the Barnsley Canal). In the background Lund Hill Lane curves away uphill towards Monckton Main Colliery and Havercroft, while on the right before the bridge is the entrance to Royston & Notton Station – not to be confused with nearby Notton & Royston. *Geoff Warnes*

The White Ladies were Arthur Rowe's only post-war double-deckers. Ribble had used them on medium-distance limited stop and express services in Lancashire; the first were Leyland PD1s, perhaps underpowered, and in 1951 they were followed by some more powerful PD2s with East Lancs bodywork of similar appearance. DCK 216 was one of the latter, joining the Cudworth-based fleet at the end of 1961. By the time of this September 1964 photograph taken in Barnsley Bus Station it was Rowe's last remaining double-decker and looks impressive as it waits to leave stand 25 for Royston. *Ken Jubb*

Rowe's fleet usually stood at about a dozen during the '50s and '60s, including coaches and contract vehicles, and as the 1960s progressed single-deckers were used more often on the stage-carriage service. One of two that came from the West Riding fleet was this 1954 Seddon Mark 11 with Duple Midland body – it seems to lack any visible indication of ownership. The other of the pair was an AEC Regal IV with a centre-entrance Roe body. The photograph dates from September 1964, a year after the bus had joined the Rowe fleet. From 1 October 1969 operation of the service passed to Yorkshire Traction, although the business survived for a few years longer. *Ken Jubb*

131

The Doncaster Independents

LEON · SELWYN · BARRAS (DON) · HOLLING · ENNIFER (BLUE ENSIGN) · FELIX MORGAN (BLUE LINE) · ROSSIE · SEVERN · STORE (RELIANCE) · WILSON (PREMIER)

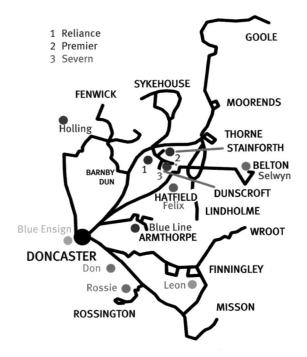

1 Reliance
2 Premier
3 Severn

GOOLE
SYKEHOUSE
FENWICK
MOORENDS
Holling
THORNE
STAINFORTH
BELTON
Selwyn
BARNBY
DUN
DUNSCROFT
HATFIELD
Felix
LINDHOLME
Blue Ensign
Blue Line
ARMTHORPE
WROOT
DONCASTER
Don
FINNINGLEY
Rossie
Leon
ROSSINGTON
MISSON

Prior to the 1920s, Doncaster was a quiet market town where the main industrial activities revolved around the huge railway works of the Great Northern Railway. The demand for coal, and improving methods for extracting it from deeper below the surface, led to the sinking of pits in the countryside around the town; small villages grew into substantial mining communities as miners moved with their families from various parts of the country to work at these new collieries.

The demand for transport grew just at the time when reliable motor vehicles were becoming available and enterprising individuals started to provide transport from the new communities to the town. Competition was rife, and the Corporation also saw opportunities in this field. It took the 1930 Road Traffic Act to regulate the situation, and some order was established.

Whilst many of the individuals had failed, a number prospered, their efforts bolstered by rapid population growth and increase in demand. There was no large company operator established in the town to squeeze them out of business. The independents flourished, mostly sharing just one or two routes and running a mix of new and second-hand vehicles, though new double-deckers became the norm for many as we moved into the 1950s and 60s.

The Christ Church terminus was a particular hotbed of independent activity. From here services ran to Armthorpe (shared by Felix, Blue Line and the Corporation), Moorends (Felix, Severn and Premier), Dunscroft (Reliance, Severn and the Corporation) and Goole (Blue Line and Reliance) as well as less frequent services to Sykehouse (Severn) and Kirkhouse Green (Reliance). At busy times operators frequently duplicated their departures. Christ Church was also the layover point for Selwyn Motors' single Saturday journey from Belton and Epworth.

A further bus station, at Marsh Gate, must be mentioned, although it was primarily served by operators based in West Yorkshire (including South Yorkshire Motors) and already covered in the Colours book of that name. Only the Saturday service of T. W. Holling from Moss and Fenwick is covered here. Most of the operators mentioned above flourished through to the end of the period covered by this book: only Don Motors had sold out (to East Midland) whilst Holling had ceased his stage carriage service.

South Yorkshire Motors was a car dealer and bus operator based in Pontefract and therefore featured in The Colours of West Yorkshire. However, they provided two hourly services into Doncaster as well as sharing a Pontefract – Barnsley service with Yorkshire Traction. Park Royal-bodied Leyland PD2/30 number 80 is standing in Doncaster's Marshgate Bus Station in 1963 prior to departing on the company's service to Leeds.
Richard Simons

Leon

Leon Motor Services had shared the Doncaster – Finningley corridor with T S Madeley of Blaxton, until January 1951 when Leon acquired that business. A significant boost to traffic occurred in the mid-50s when RAF Finningley was developed as a V-bomber base, bringing thousands of additional service personnel to the area. At this time the company relied upon the second-hand market to provide its service buses, and one such acquisition, number 33 (BLH 778), is pulling away from Doncaster Glasgow Paddocks Bus Station on 2 February 1956. Formerly London Transport STL719, it is an AEC Regent with bodywork constructed by LPTB in its own workshops. New in 1935, it was 19 years old when purchased by Leon and gave two years service before being sold for scrap. *Geoff Warnes*

The sleepy village of Misson was served by Leon buses several times per day. Whilst weekday journeys went via Finningley and supplemented the main service on that corridor, Saturday journeys ran via the most direct route to Doncaster along Bawtry Road. Bus 48 (FBW 887) is being overtaken by a tractor while it stands at the terminus alongside Misson parish church. A Daimler CVD6 with Massey bodywork, it was third-hand when acquired in 1958, having been new to Heyfordian, Upper Heyford in 1952, then passing to Ronsway, Hemel Hempstead in 1957. It was unusual in having been fitted with platform doors from new. It would remain in service with Leon until 1971. *Geoff Warnes*

The area just inside the entrance of Glasgow Paddocks bus station was often used as a layover point. On 1 June 1957 Leon 34 was waiting prior to undertaking a journey on the infrequent route to the Lincolnshire village of Wroot. It is a Daimler of chassis type TV45/2, built in 1945 as a prototype for the post-war CVD6. Fitted with Willowbrook coachwork and registered FRW 587 in Coventry, it was retained by Daimler as a demonstrator and testbed until it was sold to J W Kitchin, Pudsey in 1952. Acquired by Leon in 1955, it was used both on service work and coaching, and was withdrawn in 1962. *Roger Holmes*

The queueing traffic and line of full buses indicates that this was the day of the 1960 Battle of Britain Air Display at RAF Finningley. Leon 55 is struggling to maintain the normal service to Wroot, whilst Doncaster Corporation 123 and two buses of Premier follow behind, hired in by Leon to cope with the crowds. Wily passengers will have boarded the Wroot bus in order to pay the normal fare rather than the inflated fare on the special buses. JNU 830 was a Daimler CWD6 with Massey lowbridge bodywork, featuring a startling degree of rake to the front of the upper deck. It was new to Chesterfield Corporation in 1946, coming to Leon in 1960 and withdrawn in the following year. *Geoff Warnes.*

When Leon 57 took to the road in July 1961, it was the first new double-decker to join the fleet – the chassis (number 30000) had been on display at the 1956 Commercial Motor Show. It had been retained by Daimler for development purposes until sold to Leon and fitted with this forward entrance bodywork by Roe. Fitted with the big Daimler CD650 engine, it was an impressive vehicle and served Leon until 1978. It is pictured pulling away from Misson church. *Geoff Warnes*

In 1961 Leon also acquired a trio of second-hand Daimler double-deckers from Leicester City Transport. One of these, number 58 was standing in the spare bay in Glasgow Paddocks bus station on 9 June 1962. They were CVD6 models, with substantially-built Roberts bodywork, new in 1949 and gave Leon five years of reliable service until they were replaced by a trio of former Devon General Regent IIIs in 1966. Appearing in the background is Leon 18, a Bedford OB with Plaxton coachwork which often helped out on stage carriage work in its later years. The bus station was so called because it stood on part of a site where Lord Glasgow used to stable his racehorses. *Geoff Warnes*

In 1970 Leon added this 30ft AEC Regent V to the fleet. Formerly with City of Oxford Motor Services, it was new in 1958 with Weymann bodywork. Despite its length it had seating for only 65 passengers, who enjoyed very generous legroom. It is standing at the traffic signals at what was then known as the Gaumont corner, on the main service to Finningley which ran approximately every 20-30 minutes. Before the opening of the M18, this section of road carried a large volume of heavy goods traffic, often heading for the Humber ports. The picture date is April 1971. *Geoffrey Morant*

Another AEC Regent V of Leon Motor Services waits at the Gaumont traffic lights, on its way back from Finningley. Fleet number 79 was formerly a member of the Western Welsh fleet. Exhibited at the 1956 Commercial Motor Show, it featured handsome convertible open-top bodywork by Park Royal, though it is believed that it never ran in open-top form. A one-off in the Western Welsh fleet, it joined the Leon fleet in March 1971 and left in October 1972. *Geoff Warnes*

Selwyn

Each Saturday throughout the period covered by this book, the rearmost stand at Christ Church would be occupied by a vehicle of E. R. Dodd's Selwyn Motors, from its arrival around 10.20 until departure at 16.00. Serving the villages of Belton, Epworth and Sandtoft, the service ran unchanged from the 1930s, right through until it ceased in January 2017, latterly having to adopt a different terminal point in Doncaster due to traffic management changes. On 8 September 1960, Burlingham bodied AEC Regal I FKV 994 basks in the sunshine as it awaits the return of crew and passengers. It was new to BTS of Coventry in 1947. A Roe bodied Leyland PD2 of the Severn fleet approaches in the distance. *Geoff Warnes*

For many years Selwyn Motors also provided a market day service from Belton to Thorne. On the date of the photograph, 15 March 1967, the swing bridge over the Stainforth and Keadby Canal was closed for repair and buses were terminating on the Doncaster side of the bridge, leaving passengers to walk the quarter mile or so to the shops in Thorne. Standard Duple Vista bodied Bedford OB MWB 310 was acquired from Sims of Sheffield in 1953 when it was three years old and went on to serve Selwyn for 18 years. *Roger Holmes*

Barras (Don)

John Barras had been involved in founding Ribble Motor Services but, after a disagreement, moved to Doncaster and started a service between Doncaster and Rossington, trading as Don Motors. Following a period of competition, an arrangement was reached for the service to be shared equally with Ennifer (Blue Ensign), Morpus (Rossie) and the Corporation. In 1947 he acquired his first new double-decker, EDT 680, seen passing the end of Cantley Lane on its way to Rossington. A Leyland PD1A, it had bodywork to Leyland design, but constructed by Samlesbury Engineering. It would soon be passing the proprietor's house on Bawtry Road, where he kept the small fleet in his garden. *Geoff Warnes*

Each of the operators on the Rossington service had its own regular departure time, Don Motors having the slot at 45 minutes past each hour from Doncaster. As the population of Rossington grew, it became necessary for many departures to be duplicated, as illustrated here. The lead vehicle in this June 1961 picture is HKR 41, a 1946 Bristol K6A with Weymann bodywork, previously Maidstone & District DH189. *Roger Holmes*

The last bus to join the Don Motors fleet was VDT 94, a Leyland PD2/20 with Burlingham bodywork, bought new in 1956. It is returning from Rossington along Waterdale, with the Gaumont Cinema prominent in the background. When John Barras decided that he wished to retire, he began negotiations to sell the business to one of the other local independents, but this fell through and in April 1962 the operation and buses passed to Chesterfield-based East Midland Motor Services. Only VDT 94 was retained, allocated to Worksop depot and used on local town services there, where its highbridge layout was not too much of a hindrance. *Michael Fowler*

Holling

Doncaster's Marshgate bus station was a gloomy place in the shadow of the North Bridge, adjacent to a canal and a dogs' home. Services to Askern, Pontefract, Leeds, York and Wakefield were provided by operators already covered adequately in the 'Colours of West Yorkshire'. The only local interloper was a Saturday-only service from the villages of Fenwick and Moss, provided by T W Holling of Askern. On layover on 11 June 1961 prior to returning to Fenwick, KWU 462 was an Albion Victor FT39 with Duple coachwork, new in 1951. In the background, one of West Riding's small number of highbridge Leyland PD2s waits between trips along the main road to Askern. Behind it, the chimney is that of the former municipal power station, adjacent to Greyfriars Road tram (and later trolleybus) depot. *Roger Holmes*

Ennifer (Blue Ensign)

G H Ennifer Ltd was another operator on the Doncaster – Rossington service, win departures at 15 minutes pas each hour. Based in Bentinck Street near the town centre, the company traded as Blue Ensign and also had a thriving coaching business. In 1947 it acquired BPG 507 from a dealer. This was an AEC Q double-decker with centre-entrance bodywork by Weymann. It had been new as London Transport Q4 in 1934 but had been delicenced in 1939 and stored throughout the war. It would trundle to Rossington and back for more than four years before being sold. This remarkably good colour picture was taken on 19 September 1950. *C Carter/OnLine Transport Archive*

For a number of years the Rossington service was supplemented on four afternoons per week (not Thursday, which was half-day closing) by a short working to Church Lane in Bessacarr. This was provided by each of the operators in turn on a week-by-week basis. It would later dwindle to one journey per day, at 16.12 provided by Blue Ensign to cater for schools traffic. In this September 1961 view three Blue Ensign buses and their crews, gather in Glasgow Paddocks for a mass departure. The lead vehicle, FDT 202, is a Crossley DD42/5 with metal-framed bodywork constructed by Scottish Commercial Motors. New in 1948 the Crossley would survive until 1964. *Paul Roberts*

Doncaster Corporation had taken delivery of two 8ft-wide double-deckers (one AEC, one Daimler) in 1951. Deemed too wide for certain narrow streets in the town centre (and reputedly for the depot's automatic bus wash) they were sold off to local independents in 1955, the AEC to Blue Ensign and the Daimler to Leon. The AEC, a Regent III with Roe bodywork, is heading along Waterdale on its regular route, past the fashion shop of Mary Freemantle, a Doncaster institution. It the background a Saro bodied Leyland Tiger Cub of East Midland is pulling out of Glasgow Paddocks. The Regent would pass to a PSV driving school in 1967 and would eventually be restored to its original condition by the late Tony Peart. *Photobus*

On St Leger Day in 1960, Blue Ensign 3568 DT is plying its trade on the Rossington service. An AEC Regent V with handsome Roe forward entrance bodywork, it was a particularly impressive vehicle when it took to the road in 1959. The use of white marker paint to advertise forthcoming excursions on bus windows was a common technique used by the independents but here it is advising racegoers that the bus will pass the racecourse. A similar bus joined the fleet in 1964 and the pair remained in service until replaced by two Daimler Fleetlines in 1975. *Geoff Warnes*

Felix

Felix Motors, operating from premises at Hatfield, had a one-third share of the Doncaster – Armthorpe service, and a three-eighths share of the service to Thorne and Moorends. The basic weekday service to Armthorpe required one bus from each operator, with times rotating on a weekly basis to ensure an equal share. Each operator was free to duplicate its scheduled departures and did so at busy times. An enhanced frequency applied on Saturdays and in later days on Fridays too. Felix 26, standing at Christ Church, was an AEC Regent III with comfortable Roberts bodywork, new to Felix in 1948 and sold to Samuel Ledgard in 1961, where it continued to serve until the demise of that company in 1967. It was photographed in August 1959. *Geoffrey Morant*

Felix Motors 31 is approaching Doncaster town centre on a journey from RAF Lindholme. It is a Leyland PD2 with Leyland's own bodywork, one of two obtained new in 1950. Lindholme Aerodrome was served as part of the Doncaster – Moorends corridor, with the level of service reducing as activities at the RAF station declined in the 1960s. In later years the camp closed altogether and the site became the location for two (and recently three) prisons. *Chris Aston*

Between 1956 and 1966, Felix standardised on the AEC Regent V with Roe bodywork for its double-deck intake, with a total of eight such buses entering service during that period. As the village of Armthorpe had expanded, it was necessary for the bus service to be extended to serve different terminal points with alternate journeys. Felix 39 is standing at the Mercel Avenue turning circle, showing off the immaculate condition in which the fleet was always maintained. *Omnibus Society/Peter Henson*

A Roe bodied Daimler Fleetline of Felix Motors stands at the Moorends terminus opposite the Winning Post Hotel. There were several minor variations to the Moorends route: this bus is returning to Doncaster via Brickyards – the most direct route. Bus 52 was the penultimate addition to the fleet, new in 1972. The Duple bodied coach behind, from either the Blue Line or Reliance fleet, is probably waiting to depart on a colliers' contract, as miners were redeployed to other pits when coal production at Thorne colliery was suspended in the mid-50s due to excessive water ingress. This provided a lucrative source of work for bus and coach operators in the area for many years. *Jim Sambrooks*

Morgan (Blue Line)

Samuel Morgan began a service between Doncaster and Goole in the 1920s, trading as Gwen Motors. In 1930 he sold this business, with three buses and premises at Stainforth to Richard Wilson, who was operating between Doncaster and Armthorpe, using the Blue Line fleet name. The two businesses were merged as Samuel Morgan Ltd, trading as Blue Line. In 1949, Richard Wilson added to his empire by purchasing R. Store Ltd, which was retained as a separate entity, though operations were closely dovetailed. In 1953 the service of Majestic between Stainforth and Goole was acquired, giving the Morgan/Store empire a monopoly of services between Doncaster and Goole. For many years this service was restricted to single-deck vehicles due to a weak bridge at Rawcliffe Bridge, a situation that was not resolved until a new bridge was opened in 1967. Some time afterwards, Blue Line LWT 500 was waiting departure at Christ Church. It was a 1952 Guy Arab III with Gardner 5LW engine and bodywork constructed by Guy to Park Royal design. *Ken Jubb*

Throughout the 1950s, Blue Line favoured Guys for most of its fleet additions. Single-deckers were required for the Goole services, and an assorted collection included PWR 88, a rare combination of Guy Arab LUF chassis with Mann Egerton Sandringham coachwork, equally suitable for bus or coach work. In the reversed livery of light blue with dark blue relief more readily associated with the Reliance fleet, on 23 March 1963 it is leaving Christ Church on the service to Dunscroft shared with Severn and the Corporation. *Roger Holmes*

Richard Wilson remained an enthusiastic operator of Guy double-deckers throughout the 1960s, and between 1963 and 1967, three Arab Vs with Roe forward-entrance bodywork entered service with Blue Line. The second of these, KYG 299D, is seen approaching Doncaster's Southern Bus Station whilst operating on loan to Leon Motor Services on the Finningley service when accident damage to one of Leon's new Fleetlines caused a temporary shortage of buses. The wooden building in the background housed the Motor Vehicle Taxation Office of Doncaster County Borough, and would be closed following changes to the licensing system in 1975. *Richard Simons*

In 1968 the opportunity was taken to acquire two Leyland PD3s from the Kippax & District fleet when the Wallace Arnold group disposed of its stage carriage interests in West Yorkshire. Though decidedly non-standard, they were less than three years old when purchased and allowed for the disposal of elderly Guy Arabs. These buses were noteworthy in having illuminated offside advertisement panels between the decks, which Blue Line used to promote its own services. In the early 1970s when DUG 166C was photographed heading along Armthorpe Road, the company's phone numbers were shown as Armthorpe 230 and Stainforth 235. *Richard Simons*

Rossie

Another operator on the Doncaster – Rossington service was Rossie Motors. Started by William Morpus who had worked at Rossington Colliery, the company provided the departures at 30 minutes past each hour from Doncaster. Its buses followed a slightly different route within Rossington, taking them closer to the depot at Coxley House. The company developed a preference for Daimlers almost from the start, and adopted a livery of two shades of green and cream. Daimler CVD6 KWT 600 is standing in Waterdale prior to duplicating the company's departure on the main service. The chassis was obtained new in 1951 and originally fitted with the 1934 English Electric body from a former Hull Corporation Daimler CP6. It ran in this condition until 1954, when it was fitted with the 1949/50 Burlingham body shown, obtained from an untraced source. In this form it is shown here on 8 September 1962; it continued to serve the company until 1971. *Roger Holmes*

Standing in Glasgow Paddocks on 15 June 1960 prior to departing on yet another trip to Rossington, is MWU 750, one of the small number of Daimler CD650s sold on the home market. Having a chassis built in 1951 and retained unregistered by Daimler, it was fitted with the Burlingham body shown and sold to Rossie in 1953. Despite its foibles, it continued to serve until 1969, when it was scrapped, the engine being sold to Tailby & George (Blue Bus Services), Willington for use in one of its CD650s. *Roger Holmes*

The preference for Daimlers continued through the 1960s and after obtaining one of the last chassis fitted with Daimler's own diesel engine in 1962, the company was forced to specify a Gardner engine in BYG 890B, a CVG6/30 with Roe bodywork received in 1964. It is seen on South Parade approaching Doncaster town centre at the end of another journey on its customary route. *Richard Simons*

From 1968 the town centre terminus moved to the newly-built Southern Bus Station, which was located beneath the multi-storey car park visible on the right. Leaving with a customary good load, RYG 545L is a Daimler Fleetline, one of a pair with Roe bodies which entered service in 1972. This combination of chassis and body was becoming the standard for the majority of the area's remaining independent operators. This bus would pass to SYPTE with the Rossie Motors business in 1980, and then move on again to become Leon 106 in 1984, outside the scope of this book. *Richard Simons*

Severn

T Severn & Sons had a three-eighths share of the 'top road' service between Christ Church and Moorends, and a one-third share of the service to Dunscroft. In addition it was the sole operator of an infrequent service to Sykehouse that was restricted to single-deckers due to canal bridge weight limits. Thomas Severn had moved to Stainforth from Cresswell in Derbyshire, and had used the fleet name "Cressy" before World War 2. After the war, the fleet name was dropped and all double-deckers bought new were Leylands. KWR 359 was the last of four PD2s with Leyland bodywork when it entered service in 1951. It displays the plain green livery with one cream band which would give way during the 1960s to a version with more cream. The fleet had moved into a new purpose-built depot in Dunscroft in 1954. The picture was taken on 13 April 1963. *Roger Holmes*

In 1956 Severn updated its single-deck fleet with a pair of AEC Reliances, a surprising choice given the general preference for Leylands. With Park Royal bodywork that was finished off at the Roe factory in Leeds, they originally carried the mostly green bus livery but in 1963, one was sold and the other (PYG 605) was refurbished as a semi-coach suitable for local private hire work. On 8 June 1963 it was photographed in this form at Christ Church, loading for a journey to the village of Sykehouse, served exclusively by Severn. The journey would take it across both the Stainforth and Keadby Canal and the New Junction Canal, the latter at a swing bridge with a weight limit which precluded the use of double-deckers. *Roger Holmes*

Severn remained loyal to the post-war Leyland Titan right up to 1964, the bodywork contract switching to Roe when Leyland ceased its coachbuilding activities. From 1958 the choice was for the 30ft-long PD3, the last four deliveries having forward entrances. The final one of these, BWW 654B, is approaching Christ Church along Thorne Road in October 1969, at the end of a journey from Moorends via South Common and Brickyards. When the fleet passed to SYPTE in 1979, it served its new owner briefly and was then cut down for use as a recovery vehicle. *Geoffrey Morant.*

XWU 890G was the second Atlantean to enter the Severn fleet, in January 1969. It was fitted with an Albion Atlantean badge – these were fitted to a large batch of Glasgow buses that were on the production line at the same time. The Roe bodywork was constructed alongside a number of similar buses for Kingston-upon-Hull, and shared many of the features specified by that operator. In particular, the flat one-piece windscreen made this a very distinctive bus in the Doncaster area. *Geoffrey Morant*

149

Store (Reliance)

Robert Store started a service from Stainforth to Doncaster in the early 1920s, trading as Reliance, later adding a service through to Goole jointly with Samuel Morgan. He would sell the business to Richard Wilson, by then the owner of S Morgan Ltd in 1949, following which the two companies would remain separate entities, though working very closely together. Prior to the outbreak of World War 2, the fleet had been all single-deck, but enforced reductions to the timetable meant that double-deckers were required and Store was allocated a new Guy Arab II by the Ministry of Supply. With utility bodywork by Park Royal, EWU 374 is seen on 27 April 1957 in the shadow of the trees in the graveyard of Christ Church. It wears the reversed version of Blue Line livery adopted initially by Richard Wilson for buses in the Reliance fleet. *Roger Holmes*

Prior to his selling the business to Richard Wilson, Robert Store's livery was an unusual combination of pale green, dark blue and cream. Pictured here on 15 June 1958, JWX 261 retained this livery long after the remainder of the fleet had been repainted two shades of blue. It was one of a pair of Leyland Comets with dual-purpose coachwork by Barnaby of Hull that were delivered in 1949/50, just after the company's sale. These were capable of operating Store's infrequent service to the hamlet of Kirkhouse Green, crossing the old swing bridge over the canal at Barnby Dun. This service would be withdrawn in 1971, many years after the disappearance of the Comets. *Roger Holmes.*

In the early post-war years, both Blue Line and Reliance received new examples of the Guy Arab Mark III with bodywork built by Guy to Park Royal design. Resplendent in the predominantly light blue livery of Reliance, LWR 337 sets off from Christ Church on 23 March 1963, evidently duplicating the later Arab Mark IV in the background, as far as Stainforth. A newspaper vendor almost always used to stand on this corner – his absence from this view is puzzling. *Roger Holmes*

The service to Stainforth and Dunscroft was shared between Severn, Reliance and the Corporation. On weekdays each operator had its own regular timing and a fourth bus working was shared between the Corporation and Severn. On Saturdays an enhanced service included scheduled short workings to Barnby Dun. Busy departures were duplicated and two double-deckers of Reliance await customers at Christ Church. The lead vehicle, MNU 777 is with its third operator, having been new to Naylor of South Normanton in 1948. It subsequently passed to Trent and was acquired by Reliance in 1959. A Guy Arab III with Northern Coachbuilders bodywork, photographed on 16 May 1964 it was the last bus to receive the predominantly light blue livery before the company adopted the mainly dark blue livery of Blue Line. *Roger Holmes*

Blue Line and Reliance were quick to recognise the potential benefits when the operation of 30ft-long double-deckers was legalised in 1956. Reliance acquired TYG 4, a Guy Arab IV built to the new length in 1957 and shown here in September 1962. With Burlingham 73-seat bodywork it was otherwise very conservative, retaining an open rear platform and exposed radiator, the latter feature being very uncommon on 30ft-long Guys. *Omnibus Society/Roy Marshall.*

The last new half-cab double-deckers to enter service in the South Yorkshire area were a pair of Guy Arab Vs, one each for Blue Line and Reliance, which arrived in August 1967. The Reliance example, RWY 892F, is standing at a temporary terminus for the Goole service in Christchurch Road during a period when the normal stands at Christ Church were inaccessible due to road works. This bus met an ignominious end when in March 1979, as negotiations to sell the company to SYPTE were being concluded, it fell on to its side into a ditch on Johnny Moor Long Lane (between Moorends and Rawcliffe) and was never repaired. *Jim Sambrooks*

Wilson (Premier)

Harold Wilson was the third operator on the Doncaster – Moorends corridor, with an agreed one-quarter share of the service mileage. He had started in the early 1930s, from a base on East Lane, Stainforth, adopting the fleetname Premier. After receiving a utility Guy Arab in 1944, the company remained loyal to Guy chassis for its new double-deckers for around 20 years. Pictured here on 3 May 1958, JWR 184 was an Arab III with bodywork by Barnaby, new in 1949. Whilst in some ways it resembled the Roe product of the day in appearance, it was rather less soundly constructed and was withdrawn after ten years service. *Roger Holmes*

During the 1950s, Premier obtained a total of four tin-front Guy Arab IVs. The second of these, SWT 644 is already well-laden as it waits at Christ Church to depart to Moorends. With handsome Roe bodywork and its operator's conservative dark blue livery, it made a fine sight on 3 May 1958. It would serve Premier from 1956 through to 1970, along with a virtually similar sister bus delivered the following year. *Roger Holmes*

In 1965 the Premier fleet received its first rear-engined double-decker, in the form of HYG 123C, a new Daimler Fleetline with Roe bodywork. It was delivered in a brighter version of the livery with large areas of light blue, and more cream. Variations of this were applied to other members of the fleet in due course. The picture date is 11 August 1970. *John Kaye*

In 1973, due to an increase in contract work, Premier added two second-hand double-deckers to its fleet. The first was 7871 WJ, a former Sheffield AEC Regent V with Alexander bodywork. It was acquired from the dealer Tiger Coaches of Salsburgh, who had evidently prepared it in anticipation of a sale to one of the members of the A1 Ayrshire Bus Owners cooperative, including the fitting of platform doors. Urgently needed by Premier, it was pressed into service in A1 livery but after a very short time the rear of the bus was seriously damaged in an accident, and when it returned from repair, the new panels had received fleet livery. The remainder of the bus received fleet livery in due course and it served until 1979. *Richard Simons*

Following the new Fleetline in 1965, no further new double-deckers joined the fleet until 1973, when XWU 798L arrived. Seen approaching Christ Church in as-new condition, it was a Leyland Atlantean of the new AN68 variety, with bodywork constructed by Alexander in Falkirk. The destination blind has already been set for the following journey, to Moorends via Brickyards and the South Common Estate. *Omnibus Society/ Peter Henson*

Another second-hand purchase in 1973 was 310 MFC. An example of the integrally-constructed Park Royal/AEC Bridgemaster, it had started life with City of Oxford Motor Services in 1962 and was hurriedly acquired from Sherriff of Gainsborough. It is approaching Christ Church to work a duplicate journey on the Moorends service as far as Hatfield. By this time the fleet had expanded significantly with extensive coaching activities and contract work to Scunthorpe steelworks. *Richard Simons*

The Sheffield and Rotherham Independents

BOOTH & FISHER · DEARNEWAYS · FOSTER · WIGMORE

In contrast to Barnsley and Doncaster, there were few independently run bus services in Rotherham or Sheffield; here the municipal and major company operators had gained an almost complete monopoly by the mid 1930s.

Rotherham Corporation had bought out the last independent to run into the town (other than on colliery services) in 1935, although elsewhere in what was to become the Rotherham Metropolitan Borough in 1974 two small operators survived in Dinnington. Foster ran a short local service to Kiveton Park and Wigmore operated an hourly service to Sheffield via Thurcroft and Whiston, latterly using high-capacity single-deckers. Both operators lasted into the South Yorkshire PTE era, although Foster's service was progressively reduced, the firm ceasing trading in 1974. Wigmore, however, continued into the deregulated age of the late 1980s when new owners transformed the operation into the Northern Bus Company.

The position in Sheffield was similar, with the Joint Omnibus Committee buying out several smaller operators on the fringes of the city in the 1920s and 1930s. Of the city-based operators, only Abbey Lane Motor Services survived World War Two. Its main business was coaches and when sold to Sheffield United Tours in 1953 the only bus service, the lengthy run to New Ollerton, passed to East Midland.

One other long-standing independent continued to reach Sheffield city centre. Booth & Fisher were based at Halfway, near Killamarsh in Derbyshire, and operated approximately hourly from Sheffield to Killamarsh via Coal Aston and Eckington, while another of their services ran at a similar frequency from Beighton to Worksop via Killamarsh, Kiveton Park and Shireoaks. Sheffield's boundaries were much expanded in 1967, incorporating an adjoining area of north Derbyshire, which included both Halfway and Beighton. This had the effect of making Booth & Fisher a Yorkshire operator and from then on their new vehicles had Sheffield registrations.

A remarkable independent operation appeared on the scene in 1964, achieving a breakthrough that seemed near impossible in the highly regulated days of the 1930 Road Traffic Act. Philipson of Goldthorpe was unexpectedly granted a licence to run a regular limited-stop service between Thurnscoe and Sheffield via Goldthorpe, Wath and Rotherham, overlaying existing services provided by several of the major operators in the area, all of whom had objected. The operator used the Dearneways title and the service prospered despite the imposition of stringent restrictions on picking up and setting down (later relaxed to an extent) and the introduction of a rival service by Mexborough & Swinton.

Booth & Fisher and Dearneways survived into the PTE era – they were acquired by the PTE in 1976 and 1981 respectively.

Booth & Fisher

In addition to the two main bus services Booth & Fisher of Halfway was heavily involved in providing transport for the many local collieries. After the war the company built up a large fleet of Bedford OWBs and OBs; many lasted until the late 1960s but by then were confined to contract work. In 1948, for example, 15 new OBs were bought, all with Yorkshire-built bodies: six from Allsop of Sheffield, six from Woodall Nicholson of Halifax and three from Barnaby of Hull. Between 1956 and 1960 ten used OBs were added, with Beadle or Mulliner bodies. Apart from the Barnaby trio, all were buses and amazingly the firm never had an OB with the almost ubiquitous Duple body. This scene in the garage yard shows Mulliner-bodied GEW 58, acquired in 1958, alongside Allsop-bodied MNU 80 new in 1948 – both in use until 1968. Wales, on the blind of the leading bus, is a village about three miles away. *Tom Robinson*

Larger buses appeared in the fleet from the early 1950s, starting with two Leyland Royal Tigers bought new in 1952 and 1954. After this, the choice for heavyweight buses switched to AEC and the next were a pair of AEC Monocoaches with Park Royal bodies bought new in 1954/55. Both gave over twenty years' service. The Killamarsh – Sheffield service was only extended into the heart of the city centre in 1970 when the terminus was moved to Arundel Gate; previously it had terminated in Earl Street, a back street off the Moor. In this Arundel Gate picture the Monocoach has a duplicate in the shape of a former Maidstone & District AEC Reliance with Weymann body, one of four acquired from 1973. *Malcolm King*

157

Seven AEC Reliances were bought from 1956 to 1959, six with Roe dual-purpose bodies and the other with a Park Royal bus body which resembled the Monocoaches and came in 1957. The dual-purpose vehicles carried a mainly cream livery, as illustrated here by one of the 1959 pair working the Worksop to Beighton service. *Omnibus Society/Peter Henson*

As the Bedford OBs started to become obsolete, Albion Nimbuses were favoured, starting with a pair bought new in 1960. Ten second-hand examples followed between 1964 and 1968, including a former demonstrator and others from the Great Yarmouth, Halifax and Western Welsh fleets. This former Halifax Weymann-bodied example dated from 1963 and was acquired when only three years old. It lasted in service until 1978, by which time Booth & Fisher had been wholly owned by South Yorkshire PTE for more than two years. Here it is in Newcastle Street, Worksop, before returning to Kiveton on a short working of the Beighton service. *Omnibus Society/Peter Henson*

The 1960s brought two more bus-bodied AEC Reliances, both following the contemporary fashion in urban buses by having dual-doorways. The first came in 1961 and had Roe bodywork; after a major accident it was rebodied by Marshall. HNU 786C followed in 1965 and also had Marshall bodywork, with 'three and two' seating for 52 passengers; the resulting narrow gangway at the rear must have been a problem for the conductor on busy journeys. *Omnibus Society/Peter Henson*

After 1967, when the Sheffield city boundary was extended to include Halfway, Booth & Fisher's new vehicles had Sheffield rather than Derbyshire registrations. They included some Fords, starting with a pair of R226s with Duple (Midland) bodies but from 1972 there was a return to AEC Reliances. XWB 295M was a 51-seater with Plaxton Panorama Elite body to bus grant specification, bought new in 1973, shown here on its way from Killamarsh to Sheffield. *Omnibus Society/Peter Henson*

159

Dearneways

Dearneways' earliest underfloor-engined buses replaced double-deckers on the company's extensive colliery contract operations and, like many of the coaches in the fleet, were Leyland Royal Tigers. Among them were three 1951 buses with Willowbrook bodies which had originated with Devon General, although MTT 636 (number 48) had spent a year with Great Yarmouth Corporation Transport before coming to Yorkshire in 1964. Pictured at the depot in Goldthorpe High Street, it had been equipped for one-man operation on the Sheffield service, which started in October 1964 after numerous objections to the licence application were overcome. *Ken Jubb*

Throughout the 1960s Dearneways' service was worked by second-hand Leyland Royal Tigers and Tiger Cubs, many acquired from BET companies. This 1954 Weymann-bodied Tiger Cub was one of two acquired from Western Welsh in 1966. It was photographed in May 1969 in Houghton Road, Thurnscoe, with the shops in Shepherd Lane as a backdrop. The title "Dearne Valley Rotherham Sheffield Express Service" was prominently displayed. *Omnibus Society/Roy Marshall*

The Dearneways operation was completely transformed after 1970 with the introduction of Leyland Leopard coaches, most bought new to take advantage of the government's Bus Grant scheme. The service was also extended from its original terminus at Castlegate to Sheffield's Central Bus Station, giving it a much enhanced profile. Number 73 was this 1972 Leopard with 51-seat Plaxton bus grant coach body; it remained in the fleet until the business was sold to South Yorkshire PTE in December 1981. *Geoffrey Morant*

Foster

Foster's service between Dinnington and Kiveton Park railway station had a long history but remained relatively unknown outside the local area. It was not acknowledged in the timetable books of the major operators – Sheffield JOC's service 6 between Sheffield and Dinnington provided the same links. From the late 1950s double-deckers were generally used – lowheight ones because of the low bridge at Anston that also affected Sheffield's service. Pre- and post-war lowbridge Leyland Titans were followed by four AEC Bridgemasters. In this picture at the operator's premises are two of the second-hand PD2s – Massey-bodied HJN 836 came from Southend Corporation and all-Leyland POD 100 was new to Burton Coaches, Brixham, Devon. *Chris Aston*

A & C Wigmore

Wigmore's Dinnington to Sheffield service began in 1928 and over the years was operated by a variety of buses and coaches, some bought new and others second-hand. One of the used acquisitions was this 1951 Leyland Royal Tiger with Leyland coach body which came from the Trent fleet in 1962. In August 1964 it was at the departure stand on Platform A of Sheffield's Central Bus Station before setting off on the 50-minute run to Dinnington, with Sheffield AEC Regent V 878 behind. *Ken Jubb*

In the mid 1960s Wigmore had a change of direction and began to buy new buses, settling on the Bedford VAL in 1964 after a single SB was acquired in the previous year. HWU 402C was one of a pair bought in 1965 with 56-seat Duple Midland bodywork and all further 1960s deliveries were also VALs, latterly with Willowbrook bodies. It is pictured in September 1965 passing the stop for one of the collieries situated along the line of route from Dinnington to Sheffield through the villages of Laughton-en-le-Morthen, Thurcroft and Whiston. *Omnibus Society/Roy Marshall*

Wigmore acquired 16 Bedford VAL buses between 1964 and 1971 – most bought new and kept for only a few years before being replaced. Only one was second-hand – Duple Midland bodied AJS 110B came to industrial South Yorkshire in 1966 from a very different environment, having spent its first couple of years in the Outer Hebrides with Mitchell of Stornoway, who had bought it new in 1964. Still in Mitchell's livery, this view shows it passing Sheffield Midland Station as it begins its homeward journey to Dinnington on 17 June 1967. *Iain MacGregor*

After buying nothing but Bedford VALs for almost a decade, in 1972 Wigmore bought this Perkins-engined Seddon Pennine Mk IV with a 56-seat Seddon body. Experience with it brought a swift return to Bedfords in the form of the two-axle YRT model, with Willowbrook bodywork as on the later VALs. Here in August 1971 KWW 901K bears left from Shude Lane into Pond Street as it approaches Sheffield's Central Bus Station. Although smartly turned out in the usual blue and grey, there is no visible evidence of ownership and it was only later that Wigmore started to apply a fleetname to supplement the AWC (A & C Wigmore) logo usually found on the front of buses. *Omnibus Society/Peter Henson*

Trent

The Derby-based Trent Motor Traction Company Ltd was a BET Group company with an extensive network in Derbyshire and Nottinghamshire. Established in 1913, it had an operating area to the south of East Midland's, stretching as far as Leicester on a joint service with Midland Red. In the other direction service 64 from Nottingham extended north through Worksop to Doncaster; jointly run with East Midland (which numbered its journeys 36) it had come about through the joint 1928 takeover of Retford Motor Services.

After four decades of operation into Doncaster, Trent reached Sheffield in 1969, again on a service from Nottingham shared with East Midland. This was the X53, which ran two-hourly via Mansfield and the M1 motorway.

These services from the company's heartland were the only ones to reach Yorkshire until March 1972, when the National Bus Company transferred the Buxton and Matlock depots of the dismembered North Western Road Car Company to Trent. As a result Trent buses became a more familiar sight in Sheffield, operating the Buxton service in its entirety and sharing the Castleton service with Sheffield.

Doncaster was the northerly limit of Trent's bus network, reached by the lengthy 64 service from Nottingham. In this 1960s view 778, a 1957 Titan PD2 with Metro-Cammell body, is on the stand at Glasgow Paddocks ready to head south to Nottingham via Worksop and Ollerton – a journey of over 2½ hours. Behind is a 1961 PD3 of Yorkshire Traction, bound for Kilnhurst on service 24. *Michael Fowler*

A very different Trent double-decker, also bound for Nottingham, was 554, a 1972 Daimler Fleetline with ECW body. In this August 1972 picture, it passes Sheffield Station on its way to join City Road for the journey via Manor Top to Mosborough and Eckington and then onwards via the M1 motorway and Mansfield to Nottingham, with a running time of around one hour 40 minutes. The X53 started on 1 June 1969 and brought Trent buses to Sheffield for the first time. *Omnibus Society/Peter Henson*

The splitting of North Western led to a major expansion of Trent's territory and from March 1972 the company became involved in services between Sheffield and the Peak District. 36ft-long AEC Reliance 378, a type not previously operated by Trent, came from North Western with the Buxton operations, and is returning thence on the scenic journey via Tideswell and Millers Dale on service 184, the number used by Trent for the 84, which for many years had been jointly operated by North Western and SJOC. The date is September 1972. *Peter Henson*

A further round of NBC rationalisation saw Midland General, which had passed to the British Transport Commission in 1949, placed under the control of Trent's management. This resulted in Trent gaining a fleet of Bristol MW6Gs, some of which were moved to Buxton where the Bristol/Gardner/ECW combination was no doubt well received by the former North Western depot engineering staff. Here, in July 1972, Trent 168 approaches the departure stand in Sheffield Central Bus Station prior to a journey to Buxton. *Peter Henson*

Trent later acquired Bristols of its own, both double- and single-deck, but only a small number of ECW-bodied REs carried pre-NBC livery. Five service buses were from an outstanding North Western order while the other seven were coaches of the type illustrated here. Three were coaches while the other four were dual-purpose vehicles, fitted for one-man operation on stage-carriage services. This view shows number 270 in Central Bus Station, Sheffield, after working service X53 from Nottingham – a more comfortable vehicle for this inter-urban service than the Fleetline shown on the previous page. *John Hardey*

Chesterfield

Chesterfield is an important market and industrial town situated a little over ten miles south of Sheffield, in north Derbyshire. The corporation's involvement with local transport provision began in 1897 when it took over the locally-owned horse tramway, which it later extended and electrified. The trams were replaced by trolleybuses in 1927 but they had an even shorter life and after just eleven years motor buses took their place. Motor bus operation had begun in 1914 and in 1922 the municipalities of Sheffield and Chesterfield met the strong demand for travel between the two centres by introducing a jointly operated bus service connecting the tram termini at Woodseats (Sheffield) and Whittington Moor (Chesterfield). The service followed the main road via Dronfield and was extended over the tram tracks at each end in August 1925, creating an important interurban bus link.

This was not the only Chesterfield Corporation service into what was to become South Yorkshire. For many years a summer-only service ran to Fox House, on the Yorkshire/Derbyshire boundary, and from 1962 the corporation was a joint operator with East Midland and Sheffield of services 62 and 64 between Chesterfield and Sheffield via Eckington.

Chesterfield Corporation Transport outlived the South Yorkshire municipal operators, surviving until it was sold to its management and employees in 1990, although the long established green and cream livery disappeared during the 1980s.

Chesterfield invested heavily in new double-deckers immediately after the war, taking more than 50 from Crossley, Daimler and Leyland in 1946/47. Next to arrive, in 1950, were 20 Guy Arab IIIs with Weymann side-gangway bodywork. They included 180, seen here during its first year of operation at Central Bus Station, Sheffield, before returning to its home town on service 12. The angle of this view shows the longer bonnet required by the Gardner 6LW engine. *C Carter*

Service 12 from Sheffield to Chesterfield followed the A61 through Meadowhead, Dronfield and Unstone, and operation was shared by the Sheffield JOC, from its inception in 1929, and Chesterfield Corporation. Chesterfield 192, one of a dozen Daimler CVG6s with Weymann bodywork bought in 1955/56, passes Graves Park in Sheffield on the steady climb from Heeley through Woodseats to Meadowhead, heading south for Chesterfield. The red W below the driver's cab denotes an eight-foot wide bus before this became the norm. *Martin Llewellyn*

Until 1957 all double-deckers had been of lowbridge configuration with side gangways, but in that year the first of many Leyland PD2s entered service, with highbridge bodywork by Weymann. As there were still many low bridges on the system, they had to be carefully allocated, but by 1960 there were 34 of them. Some, like the 1960 bus seen here, were fitted with platform doors for use on out-of-town services. In this August 1967 photograph, 231 was in Sheaf Street, immediately after leaving Sheffield's Central Bus Station for the 49-minute run back to Chesterfield. *Geoffrey Morant*

Chesterfield's first rear-engined double-deckers, four lowbridge Leyland Atlanteans, came in early 1960. After another batch of Titans four Daimler Fleetlines were added in 1962/63, but these too were followed by more front-engined vehicles, this time Daimler CCG6s. Metro-Cammell bodied 304 was one of the Fleetlines, shown here leaving Sheffield's Pond Street on service 512, a limited-stop service to Chesterfield with just five intermediate stops and no setting down before Dronfield on journeys from Sheffield. *Iain MacGregor*

In late 1963 ten single-deckers with 42-seat Park Royal dual-door bodies were placed in service. Two were on Leyland Leopard L1 chassis; the others were AEC Reliances. In this May 1968 picture, 24 is at the terminus of the summer-only service 7 to Fox House, where connections were advertised with the Sheffield – Castleton service operated by North Western and the Sheffield JOC. The historic Fox House Inn is in the background, while the bus faces towards Owler Bar ready for the scenic return journey through Barlow to Chesterfield. *Omnibus Society/Peter Henson*

Like several other municipals Chesterfield had a small coach fleet and in August 1973 acquired this Bedford YRQ with Willowbrook 002 bodywork. In order to qualify for the government bus grant it had to achieve a certain level of mileage on one-man operated stage-carriage services and is seen here in Sheffield's Central Bus Station with a destination blind which fails to indicate which service it is operating; the limited-stop 512 is perhaps the most likely as the all-stops 12 remained a double-deck stronghold. *Omnibus Society/Peter Henson*

North Western

The Stockport-based North Western Road Car Company Ltd was established in 1923 to continue one of British Automobile Traction's earliest bus-operating ventures. Its main operating area was north Cheshire and the fringes of Manchester but also included much of the Peak District, from depots in Buxton (with a small outstation in Castleton) and Matlock. The double-deck fleet used in more populous areas never ventured here and typical BET single-deckers were the norm after the large fleet of Bristol Ls had gone.

North Western reached Sheffield on service 72 from Castleton and the 84 from Buxton. Both had been inaugurated by Hancock of Bamford, who sold his bus operations to Sheffield Corporation in 1927. North Western became a joint operator in 1928, with the Sheffield Joint Omnibus Committee taking over from the corporation in 1929.

The company also operated between Sheffield and Manchester. Service 39 via the Snake Pass was a joint operation with Sheffield, the 48 via Woodhead was operated only by Sheffield until it passed briefly to North Western as the X48, while the X72 was an extension of some journeys on the 72 to Manchester via Chapel-en-le-Frith. Jointly with Yorkshire Traction, it also ran some journeys on the Manchester to Barnsley services.

In the first quarter of 1972 the SELNEC PTE took over most of North Western's services within the PTE's area and the remainder were transferred to adjacent National Bus Company subsidiaries Crosville and Trent, the latter taking the Derbyshire operations.

Service 39 connected Sheffield and Manchester via the Snake Pass and Glossop, the shortest route between the two cities, and was operated by North Western and Sheffield. The pass was often closed in winter, and the 39 only ran during the summer months. In August 1963, seven-year-old Tiger Cub 651 with BET-style Weymann body is at the Snake Inn, a little below the 1,680-feet summit of the pass on the Sheffield side, where a brief stop was scheduled. The destination blind indicates the terminus at Lower Mosley Street, Manchester. *John Law collection*

The two-hourly 84 between Sheffield and Buxton had an end-to-end journey time of just under 1¾ hours and for many years North Western and SJOC operated alternate journeys. In later days 957, a 1963 Leyland Leopard with Alexander Y-type body, is pictured in Foolow, between Tideswell and Eyam, bound for Sheffield. When SJOC was wound up at the end of 1969 the service became wholly operated by North Western but in March 1972 it passed to Trent (along with the coach and Buxton depot). *Martin Llewellyn*

East Midland

East Midland Motor Services Ltd was registered in 1927 as the successor to W T Underwood Ltd, which had close ties to Darlington-based United Automobile Services. Originally there were extensive operations in Lincolnshire but these were given up in the late 1920s, after which the head office was relocated from Clowne to Chesterfield and the company's operating area became recognisable as the one that survived into the National Bus Company era. The East Midland title was a little misleading as operations were focussed on the north-eastern extremities of the Midlands, across the coalfield areas of north-east Derbyshire and north Nottinghamshire, and spilled over into the West Riding of Yorkshire. Depots were located at Chesterfield, Clowne, Mansfield, Retford and Worksop. In fact the services into Doncaster, Rotherham and Sheffield were more important to East Midland than the tentacles that stretched south to Derby and Nottingham, and the company had joint operating agreements with Doncaster and Rotherham corporations and the Sheffield Joint Omnibus Committee, resulting in a few limited operations entirely within Yorkshire.

On the disbanding of Tilling and British Automobile Traction in 1942 East Midland transferred to the BET group and in the years which followed most buses were AECs and Leylands of typical BET appearance. A long-standing link to the company's earlier ownership was the very distinctive livery of chrome yellow with cream and brown relief, which had also been used in its early years by United. In these striking colours no-one could mistake an East Midland bus and the mid-1950s switch to a drab red seemed to rob the company of much of its individuality.

Prior to the Second World War two 1932 AEC Regents and 16 Leyland Titans dating from 1935-38 were East Midland's only double-deckers. The 1935/36 TD4s originally had Leyland lowbridge bodies; they were rebodied after the war, D14 by Roberts after suffering fire damage in 1946 and the rest by Willowbrook in 1949. On 28 August 1952 and with its new 55-seat lowbridge body, D13 is seen at Glasgow Paddocks, Doncaster, ready to work service 2 to Retford via Bawtry and Ranskill, along what was then still the Great North Road. *C Carter*

The late pre-war and early post-war years saw a complex programme of body exchanges, perfectly encapsulated by K12, a 1947 AEC Regal with a 1952 Willowbrook body. Originally numbered A12, it had begun life with a 1936 Leyland body which until 1939 was fitted to a Tiger TS7 chassis. When the Tiger was rebodied by ECW in 1939 the Leyland body was moved to a 1931 Regal chassis, and when this was withdrawn in 1947 it was transferred to the new Regal. Five years later A12 was one of 14 postwar Regals fitted with new 35-seat forward-entrance Willowbrook bodywork to form a new K class. In April 1956 it was at Glasgow Paddocks, operating a short journey to Worksop via Tickhill on service 36, with the Trent double-decker behind on the same jointly-operated service showing the Trent number (64). *Geoff Warnes*

Between 1947 and 1950 41 Leyland Titans with Leyland lowbridge bodywork were bought: two PD1s, followed over the next three years by 39 PD2/1s. This 1956 picture shows D73, built in 1949, at Glasgow Paddocks before leaving for Tickhill via Bawtry and Bircotes on service 21. By now the traditional colours were being replaced but already the livery had been simplified by painting over the cream band below the top-deck windows. *Geoff Warnes*

Leyland met East Midland's single-deck requirements during the 1950s, starting with 20 Leyland Royal Tigers in 1952. The rest were Tiger Cubs but only the 25 with Saunders-Roe bodies delivered in 1954 were in yellow/brown livery. The adoption of a deep red with ivory relief seemed to change the character of the company. Even so, R330 looks well presented in this July 1961 view at Glasgow Paddocks in Doncaster, before the lengthy run to Nottingham on service 36, which would take almost 2¾ hours. *Geoff Warnes*

The last of a long line of Leyland Titans, all lowbridge, were 12 PD3s with Weymann bodies supplied in 1957/58. Lowbridge PD3s were a rarity in BET fleets; the only others were two supplied to James of Ammanford. D127 came in 1958, and is shown here leaving Doncaster with the intriguing destination of Glass Bulbs Factory. This was run by Harworth Glass Bulbs Ltd and operated round the clock, requiring service 133 to run every eight hours, seven days a week. This was the 1.15 pm journey, timed for the two o'clock shift change; the return working from the factory on Snape Lane, Harworth, was at 2.10. *Ken Jubb collection*

After the PD3s East Midland switched to lowbridge Leyland Atlanteans between 1959 and 1961 and then to Alexander-bodied Albion Lowlanders in 1962/3. More Atlanteans came in 1965 before the last front-engined double-deckers, four more Lowlanders in 1966 – with 18 East Midland had BET's largest fleet of them. New in 1963, D172, leaves Doncaster Southern Bus Station for Harworth in the brighter version of the livery with cream lower-deck window surrounds. On layover is one of Doncaster Corporation's five Seddon Midibuses. *Malcolm King*

The L class consisted of 53-seat single-deckers delivered from 1963 to 1966; the first four were AEC Reliances and the rest were Leyland Leopards. L434 was one of nine with Weymann bodywork new in 1966 in this livery with more ivory than red – normally a bold fleetname in large capital letters would have been displayed. It is seen here tackling the steep climb up Gleadless Road as it heads out of Sheffield with a good load. The 1960s housing in Gleadless Valley is at the bottom of the hill with distant views to Crookes and beyond. Operation of service 99 to Chesterfield via Ridgeway, Marsh Lane and Barrow Hill was shared with Sheffield JOC. *Barry Ridge*

Over the twelve years between 1959 and 1971 East Midland bought 53 Leyland Atlanteans of two distinct styles – the early ones to 1961 had Weymann bodywork, while later examples from 1965 had Alexander bodywork. D197, one of the final five from 1971, picks up in Central Bus Station, Sheffield, in June 1972 bound for Mansfield and Nottingham on service X53 (displayed here as 53X). Jointly worked by East Midland and Trent, this was a new fast service introduced in June 1969, which made use of the M1 motorway between junctions 29 and 30. *Ken Jubb collection*

In late 1971 NBC influence became increasingly clear when five Bristol VRs arrived, the first Bristol double-deckers since a K5G was allocated in 1941. Throughout the 1970s VRs came in quantity but only this first batch carried BET-style red and cream; later examples arrived in NBC leaf green. Here D101 passes Sheffield Midland station at the start of a service 3 journey to Mansfield (the driver has failed to change the blind); the journey of about one hour 35 minutes would take it through Eckington, Clowne and Bolsover. Service 3 was notable in being operated in the company's own right, independently of the Sheffield JOC, which had an involvement in nearly all the inter-urban bus services from the city. *Omnibus Society/Peter Henson*

Lincolnshire

The Lincolnshire Road Car Company's bus network did not extend into South Yorkshire until 1950, when the acquisition of Enterprise & Silver Dawn included the latter's routes into Doncaster. The main services ran from Scunthorpe via the Isle of Axholme and across the sparsely-populated flatlands east of Doncaster. From January 1970, Lincolnshire buses also reached Sheffield, when the company assumed responsibility for operating a large share of service 85 from Gainsborough, formerly the domain of the Sheffield Joint Omnibus Committee.

By the 1950s services 104/106 to Scunthorpe via the Isle of Axholme were usually operated by a Bristol Lodekka. Whilst most buses ran the full route, occasional journeys terminated on the Isle at Haxey, where connections would be available for Scunthorpe and Gainsborough. For a long period Lincolnshire outstationed a bus in Doncaster; for several years it was stabled in the yard of the Lonsdale Hotel until, following the formation of the National Bus Company, it was relocated to the Yorkshire Traction depot on Milethorn Lane. 2321 was a 1955 LD6B with a Bristol 6-cylinder engine: for later deliveries the 5-cylinder Gardner was considered adequate. *Geoffrey Morant*

Another infrequent service was Lincolnshire's 156 between Scunthorpe and Thorne. When this photograph was taken in 1967, the canal bridge in Thorne was closed for repair and buses were terminating outside the Rising Sun Inn. The bus is one of the company's large fleet of Bristol SC4LKs, renowned for their economy of operation, but the route would soon be abandoned without replacement due to falling receipts. On the far side of the road, Selwyn Motors' Bedford OB awaits passengers for its service to Belton. *Michael Fowler*

West Riding

Though based in Wakefield and covered thoroughly in *The Colours of West Yorkshire*, the West Riding Automobile Company's buses played an important role in the south of the county. They need brief mention here as the company was the most frequent user of Doncaster's Marshgate bus station and for a short time had a depot in the town, inherited from Bullock & Sons in 1950 and closed a few years later. Services ran north out of the town along the A1 and A19, to Leeds, Pontefract, York and Askern. West Riding buses also served Barnsley and reached Sheffield on the long Service 67 from Leeds. In later years it was a partner in the White Rose Express network, linking South and West Yorkshire via the M1.

In a typical scene at Doncaster Marshgate bus station on 2 June 1961, two smart highbridge Leyland PD2s from West Riding's Selby garage lay over between trips to Askern. The front one, 653 (BHL 800) almost hides a Roe-bodied PD2 of South Yorkshire Motors on its service to Leeds. To the right North Bridge Road rises up over the arches to carry the Great North Road over the main east coast railway line. The four storey building in the background was in use as a lodging house and has the name "Bridge Hostel" painted on its roof. *John Kaye*

One of West Riding's ill-fated Guy Wulfrunians is approaching Sheffield Central Bus Station at the end of its 2 hour 20 minute journey from Leeds via Wakefield and Barnsley, a service shared with Yorkshire Traction and Sheffield JOC. New in 1962, 942 would serve the company for a little over six years before returning to South Yorkshire one last time – to the yard of one of the Barnsley area bus dismantlers. *Graham Hague*